WHITCHURCH

TOWNSHIP

WHITCHURCH
TOWNSHIP

Stoddart

A BOSTON MILLS PRESS BOOK

Researched and written by the Whitchurch History Book Committee:
Jean Barkey, Gordon Dibb, Karen Brooks Earley, Karen Edwards, Marjorie Richardson,
Helen Roberts, Lynne Rubbens, Robert Staley.
Published with the assistance of the Ontario Heritage Foundation

FOR MARJORIE E. RICHARDSON, 1911–1991,
historian, genealogist, and friend.
Her spirit, humour, wisdom, and generosity enriched the lives of everyone
she met. Without her this book could not have been compiled. We are
grateful to her and remember her with love and affection.

Canadian Cataloguing in Publication Data

Whitchurch Township

ISBN 1-55046-098-6

1. Whitchurch - Stouffville (Ont.) - History.
I. Whitchurch History Book Committee.

FC3095.W55W55 1993   971.3'54   C94-930058-6
F1059.W55W55 1993

© 1993 Whitchurch History Book Committee

First published in 1993 by
Stoddart Publishing Co. Limited
34 Lesmill Road
Toronto, Canada
M3B 2T6
(416) 445-3333

A BOSTON MILLS PRESS BOOK
The Boston Mills Press
132 Main Street
Erin, Ontario
N0B 1T0

Design by Mary Firth
Printed in Canada

The publisher gratefully acknowledges the support of the Canada Council,
Ontario Ministry of Culture and Communications, Ontario Arts
Council, and Ontario Publishing Centre in the development of writing
and publishing in Canada.

Front cover photo: *Strawberry festival at Bethesda.* Back cover: *Barn-raising feast.*
Title page photo: *Gertrude Nighswander, Musselman's Lake beach, 1902.*
All courtesy Whitchurch-Stouffville Museum.

❧ CONTENTS ❧

PREFACE

In 1989 a group of people working or living in the Town of Whitchurch-Stouffville came together to research and compile historical information about the community. Since Whitchurch-Stouffville had been in existence as a municipality only since 1971 with the creation of the Regional Municipality of York, the group decided that the original Township of Whitchurch would be the focus for this research. At that time no publications existed that examined the historical development of the settlement of Whitchurch. Accordingly, this lack helped to identify the main purpose of the book that we hoped would result from our research.

We produced a rough outline for the book, identifying major sections or chapters. The chapters included the physical geography and geology of the area, its archaeological and aboriginal history, the historical use of the forests and the area's early sawmills, the political development of Whitchurch, and the history of the many hamlets and towns making up the Township of Whitchurch.

As we met, discussed, and wrote, several guidelines were set up to narrow our focus and help maintain consistency through the writing. This narrower focus came about as we realized that we could not be all things to all people. We were not writing the definitive history of Whitchurch, but were rather doing the groundwork and setting the stage for those who we hoped would pick up where we left off and continue to research and write about Whitchurch.

Since Newmarket, Aurora, Stouffville, and the Oak Ridges–Bond Lake area had been previously researched and written about, we decided that we would include them as part of Whitchurch's history but not delve into their development extensively. More information about these communities is easily located. For suggestions, see the Bibliography at the end of this book.

We also decided that what we were really researching and writing about was the history of the settlement of the township. We wanted to point out some of the factors affecting the location of settlement (e.g., resources and transportation), the cultural influences, and the development of the individual communities within Whitchurch. We wanted to include the location of each community, when it was settled and why, the origins of the original settlers, and how the community developed. We would also point out any remnants of the original community still in existence. The reader will notice that all measurements included in the description of the settlement of Whitchurch are Imperial. The conversions to metric are: 1 acre equals 0.40 hectares, and 1 mile equals 1.6 kilometres.

Additionally, we identified areas that we did not want to include, perhaps because they were large topics meriting separate study, or because they did not fall within our parameters for discussion. For example, we did not examine the rural and agricultural development and history of Whitchurch. We also did not delve into genealogical history.

This book could not have been published without the financial assistance of the Ontario Heritage Foundation, the Friends of the Whitchurch-Stouffville Museum, and the Whitchurch-Stouffville Historical Society. Archaeological research was also supported by grants from the Ontario Heritage Foundation.

We would also like to acknowledge the support and assistance of the following groups and individuals, whose participation facilitated our work: Jean Barkey; Ella Barry; Russell Beare; William Brown; Robert Burgar; Lavergne Butcher; Peta Daniels; Kathy D'Andrea; William Devins; Patricia Dibb; Bill Earley (photography); Leonard Glover; Earl Goforth; Marjory Holden; Mary Hopkins; Arthur Horn; Ken Hoshel; Jeff Johnson, Town of Whitchurch-Stouffville; Beatrice Johnston; Helen Johnston; Anne Keenlyside; Cheryl Ligetti; Murielle Macia; Gordon Mackey; J.H. McAndrews; Mary MacDonald; David Mallinson; Jim Mason, editor, *Stouffville Sun*; Thomas McGreevy; W. McKinley; Laura Peers; Richard Preston; Grace Pugh; Gordon Ratcliff; Terry Ratcliff; Arthur Roberts; Ursula and Alf Ronneberger; Michael Rosen, Ministry of Natural Resources; Beth Sinyard, curator, Elman W. Campbell Museum; Alma Stephens; Peter Storck; David Stothers; Marvin Stothers; Jacqueline Stuart, curator, Aurora Museum; Elgin Toole; Janet and Peter van Nostrand; Whitchurch-Stouffville Museum Board; Andrea Wilson, curator, Whitchurch-Stouffville Museum; J.V. Wright; Joe Wright; York Regional Police.

A special thank-you to Helen Roberts for her many long and extra hours of work at the computer. A note of appreciation to Bill Earley and Karen Brooks Earley who researched and completed preliminary maps.

We wrote this book for students, for local residents, and for anyone who is curious about the history of Whitchurch. We hope that both new and long-term residents will learn something new about the area where they live.

CHAPTER 1

THE NATIVE PEOPLE

De Rottenburg map, 1850, including Whitchurch Township (note native trails).
National Museums Canada

Prior to about eleven thousand years ago, it was impossible for human groups to have taken up residence in southern Ontario. With the retreat of the ice sheet, as a result of global warming, plant and animal communities began colonizing the newly deglaciated regions, and in their wake followed small bands of early hunters. In describing human settlement in Whitchurch Township, we must examine our knowledge of its inhabitants from the earliest hunters to the Euro-American settlers.

At the time of the arrival of the first Euro-American settlers, there were at least three native trail systems still in use in Whitchurch Township: one trail paralleled Yonge Street, a second (the Vandorf Trail) ran from the headwaters at the Rouge system to Newmarket and Holland Landing, crossing the height of land at Vandorf, and the third (the Rouge Trail) ran northwest from Musselman's Lake.

Early evidence of the historic use of these native trails includes two crosses or religious ornaments from the course of the Rouge Trail. In the sixth concession of Whitchurch, a bronze crucifix bearing the inscription *Souvenir de Mission* was reportedly found along a section of the Rouge Trail on the former Skinner farm, and a similar religious ornament was also found in the 1950s farther north along the same trail on the Swezie farm at Holland Landing. Both of these items probably date from the period when the French occupied the area prior to the 1760s.

The Mississauga claim to portions of Whitchurch are on record from the time of the very first attempt by Euro-American settlers to take up residence in the township. In 1794 William Bond filed a complaint with Lt.-Gov. John Graves Simcoe, which stated that on receiving his grant along Yonge Street he sent a man to his lot in order to begin making improvements. Bond's hired help was clearing land near Bond Lake when he was visited by "three Mississaugas or Chippewas." After an altercation he was forced to return to York, minus both his provisions and the shirt from his back.

Because the Yonge Street Trail was close to Bond Lake, it is entirely possible that the three natives considered Bond's hired help to be a trespasser on traditional land, so perhaps they were merely evicting him from an area where he was not welcome. In 1796 Wabikinine, the head chief of the Credit River band of Mississaugas, visiting York, was assaulted by a soldier and two white settlers. He later died as a result of his injuries. The Wabikinine murder, coupled with the incident at Bond Lake, evidently created sufficient fear among the local white population that action was initiated to protect York from possible attack by the Mississaugas from the Lake Simcoe area. A settlement to be known as Windham was originally planned for development along the east side of Cooks Bay, but seeing the potential for native discontent, the authorities at York changed their minds about the location of Windham and placed it along Yonge Street at Oak Ridges. French royalist settlers arriving at the time of the French Revolution requested a land grant, and were given a parcel at Windham to serve as a buffer to a feared native attack on York.

Timothy Street trading tree in Newmarket.
Gordon Dibb

Considerable evidence throughout the nineteenth century indicates that the native population never totally abandoned their hunting and trapping grounds in Whitchurch. In Newmarket, tradition holds that the "trading tree" was a regular site of barter between local whites and the resident native population. Along the second concession, about 1½ miles south of the Timothy Street trading tree, was a Mississauga encampment on the former Stephens property. At this site archaeologists found quantities of bottle glass that been manufactured into woodworking tools. According to E.W. Trewhella's history of Newmarket, this area continued to be visited by natives until the late nineteenth century. There was apparently a mission church and burial ground in lot 89, concession 1, where both natives and whites were interred. The area was also possibly used for native ceremonies such as powwows by inhabitants of Rama (in the Lake Couchiching area) who came regularly to pay their respects to relatives buried in the church graveyard.

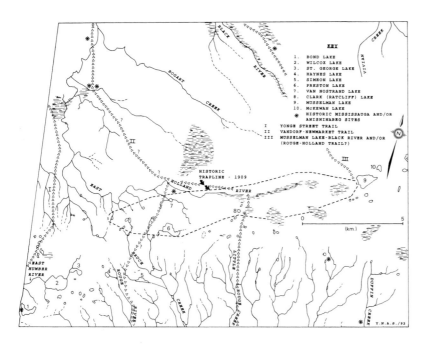

Anishinabeg trapline and native trail sites in Whitchurch.
York North Archaeological Services

Graves of whites were removed from the cemetery sometime before 1950, but the native graves are still present on the property, which is now in danger of being destroyed by urban expansion within the Town of Newmarket. Closer to Stouffville are two known cemeteries used by the Mississaugas in the nineteenth century. A native cabin may have stood near one of the Rouge headwater streams immediately adjacent to the Ratcliff Late Iroquoian village site. Here a number of worked-bottle-glass scrapers have been found, along with a very small number of nineteenth-century historic artifacts. On the Bartholomew mill property, near the railway tracks in Stouffville, native families are thought to have set up encampments in the nineteenth century, making baskets and selling them to the local villagers.

On the Michael van Nostrand property at Vandorf, one or two native families occupied a small encampment during the late nineteenth and early twentieth centuries. The encampment was in the small field north of van Nostrand Lake, and the water supply was the small outlet creek. The dwellings are considered to have been teepees made of canvas, probably from old army tents. For the most part the Mississaugas came to trade moccasins, maple sugar, baskets, glass beadwork and miniature birchbark canoes with the local white settlers. One of the last visits to the area was recorded by the late F.H. van Nostrand in 1909, when two natives came down from Georgina Island to trap. The figure on this page shows the territory covered by their trapline in central Whitchurch in 1909. Animals trapped that year included muskrats, foxes and weasels.

In 1923 Whitchurch was finally ceded by the south-central Ontario Mississaugas as part of the Williams Treaty. Prior to this date only a very small section of the extreme southwestern corner of the township had ever been legally ceded by treaty. Included in the Williams Treaty was most of northern York and Ontario counties, "almost half of the City of Toronto, to say nothing of Whitby, Oshawa, Port Hope, Cobourg and Trenton." The purchase price was $500,000, to be divided among 1328 natives (663 Mississaugas and 665 Chippewas). For the purchasing party, this was a most advantageous transaction, considering what the land was really worth in 1923.

CHAPTER 2

FROM WHITCHURCH TO WHITCHURCH-STOUFFVILLE

The Township of Whitchurch, comprising 59,743 acres, was originally located in the District of Nassau, which contained all the territory north of Lake Ontario from the Bay of Quinte to a spot intersecting Long Point in Lake Erie. In 1791 Upper Canada was created by the Constitutional Act, and the first lieutenant-governor of the new province, Col. John Graves Simcoe, assumed the position in 1792. Simcoe immediately renamed the four districts of Upper Canada, changing the District of Nassau to the Home District. In addition, he divided Upper Canada into nineteen counties, one of which was named York. The Home District as a unit of local government was altered when Toronto was incorporated as a city in 1834. At this time the City of Toronto became politically separate from the County of York.

When it was created, York County's extensive area was divided into two ridings, East and West York. In 1798 the East Riding included the townships of Whitby, Pickering, Scarborough, York, Etobicoke, Markham, Vaughan, King, Whitchurch, Uxbridge, and Gwillimbury, and an area of land that was to be later divided into townships, lying between today's counties of Durham and Lake Simcoe. It was this East Riding that evolved into the County of York.

The original boundaries of the Township of Whitchurch were different from those in use today. The northern boundary, which has not changed, was Davis Drive. Yonge Street formed the western boundary, Stouffville/Gormley Sideroad the southern, and the eastern boundary remains today as Durham Road 30. These boundaries included not only the village of Stouffville, but also present-day Newmarket, Aurora, and Oak Ridges.

Settlers arrived in Whitchurch Township as early as 1794. Indeed, some of the first settlers were squatters, who obtained squatters' rights at the time of the first survey: settlers were allowed to retain the land where they had been unlawfully living. The first surveyor of the entire township was John Stegman. His survey began in 1800 and was

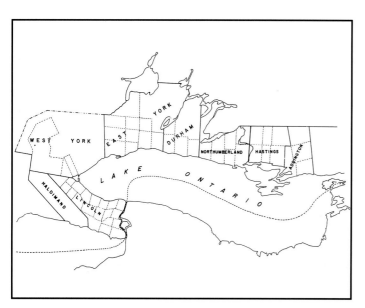

Municipal divisions c. 1798 (simplified).
The Regional Municipality of York

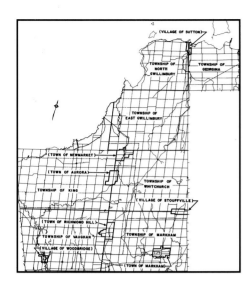

LEFT: Political boundaries (prior to 1971).
The Regional Municipality of York

BELOW LEFT AND RIGHT: Home District Townships between Lake Ontario and Lake Simcoe, c. 1799, Upper Canada Office of the Surveyor General.
Archives of Ontario

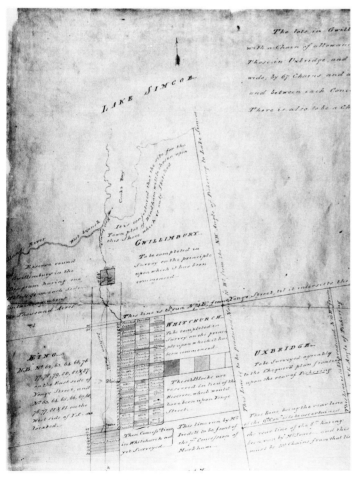

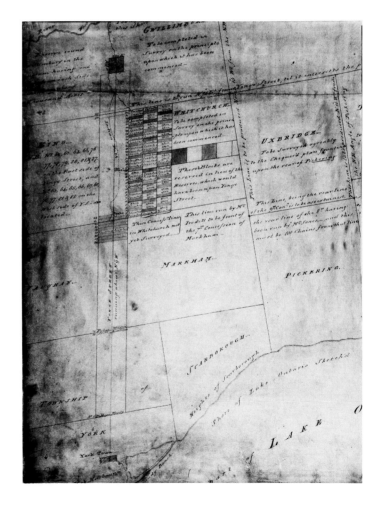

completed in 1802. Partial surveys of the first few concessions of the township had been completed earlier.

Stegman was an officer in a Hessian Regiment during the American War of Independence. Hessian soldiers, most of whom were either Dutch or German, were mercenaries employed by the British army to fight alongside British regulars. In payment for his survey work, John Stegman received 1200 acres of land in the third concession.

The survey divided Whitchurch into lots, concessions, concession roads, and sideroads. The north-south roadways were called concession roads. The strip of land between concession roads was termed a concession. Each concession was divided into 200-acre lots. Lots extended from one concession road to the next. Sideroads ran east to west, occurring every five lots. Lots were described in relation to concession roads, fronting on the westernmost boundary concession road. This means that lot 4, concession 3, refers to a 200-acre parcel of land that fronts on concession road 3, but that is also bounded by concession road 4.

Additional surveys were made by Surveyor Wilmot, and in 1869 a resurvey was conducted by John Shier. The actual date of naming the township is unknown: however, Lieutenant-Governor Simcoe chose the name to commemorate the birthplace of Lady Simcoe in Herefordshire, England.

Before settlement occurred, one-seventh of the land was set aside for clergy reserves, and an additional one-seventh for Crown reserves. Although the rental of the clergy reserve land was originally to be used for the support of the Church of England, all Protestant denominations in Upper Canada benefited. Crown reserves were also rented, the monies earmarked for the colonial administration and the aristocracy at York. Both clergy and Crown reserves were sold between 1820 and 1845.

Timothy Rogers, a Quaker from Vermont, was responsible for the settlement of forty mostly Quaker (Society of Friends) families in Whitchurch. Rogers acted as a land agent for the Upper Canadian government, which viewed the Quakers as people with the skills and abilities needed for settlement in Whitchurch. They were to move as a group and work together to help establish a viable community, which would in turn encourage others to settle in the same area. Rogers was offered one thousand acres in 1801 if he could bring in a set number of people and sell a certain number of farm lots. The forty families Rogers persuaded to locate in Whitchurch came from Vermont, New York, and Pennsylvania.

The first settlers to the township came from assorted backgrounds, choosing the area for a variety of reasons. Some were Quakers from Pennsylvania. Some Quaker families settled here for religious freedom, while others were attracted by grants of land. Hessian soldiers received land in Whitchurch as payment for their participation on behalf of the British government in the American War of Independence. Frederic Baron de Hoen was one such officer who received extensive grants in Whitchurch totalling 2600 acres. Some of the earliest settlers were French Huguenots who left France at the time of the French Revolution. Many of those who settled in the southeast part of the township, especially around the present town of Stouffville, were Mennonites.

Towards the end of the eighteenth century, the first patents for land in the township were granted. Joseph Bouchette received the first in 1796. The following year Frederic Smith, Charles Fathers, and James Pitney received their grants, and in 1798 William Bond, John Chisolm, and Capt. W. Graham came to Whitchurch. Captain Graham held 3000 acres, including lots 76 and 77 on concession 1 (Yonge Street), where he resided. Along with Timothy Rogers's group of settlers, other Quaker leaders to settle in the township included Amos Armitage and Jacob Lundy. Some of the first patentees were those who received lands by statutory right as United Empire Loyalists, government officials, or those who provided military service. Many of these people chose not to move to the lands granted them, but instead wished to sell them for as much as possible.

Settlement in Whitchurch was often clustered around waterways, fertile land, and timber resources. The Oak Ridges moraine also influenced the pattern of settlement. Small villages or hamlets were found either north or south of this ridge of high land, which crosses the township east to west.

From Census of Whitchurch Township, 1861.

Whitchurch-Stouffville Public Library

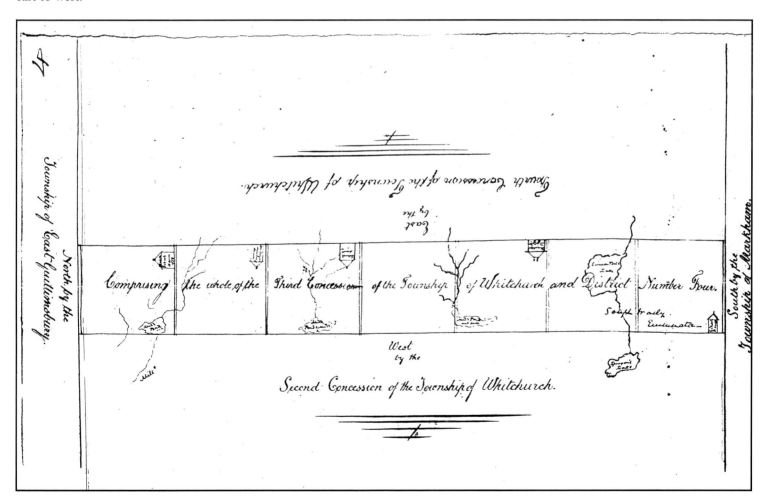

The Oak Ridges are an extensive belt of sandy and gravelly hills stretching from the Orangeville area to Rice Lake, forming the watershed between Lake Ontario and Lake Simcoe. Here one finds the sources of the streams that become the tributaries of the Don, the Rouge, or the Holland rivers. The countryside abounds in small lakes such as Wilcox Lake (originally Lake Willcocks) and Bond Lake in Oak Ridges, Preston Lake (originally Lake Reesor), Musselman's Lake, as well as many smaller lakes and ponds.

The glaciers that were responsible for forming the moraine also left behind granite float boulders throughout the area. These rocks were used extensively by early settlers as the chief building material for the foundations of houses, schools, and barns.

Early in the development of Whitchurch, small communities sprang up at various locations throughout the township: Vandorf, Bogarttown, Ballantrae, Pine Orchard, Bloomington, Gormley, Lemonville, Bethesda, Vivian, Cedar Valley, Pleasantville, and others. The sites for these hamlets were usually at the intersections of a main road, and/or near a stream or river offering a source of power for a local mill. As a community was built up around

BELOW LEFT: Oak Ridges Moraine
BELOW RIGHT: Political boundaries (1986).
The Regional Municipality of York

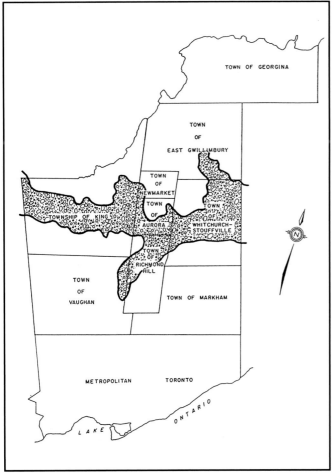

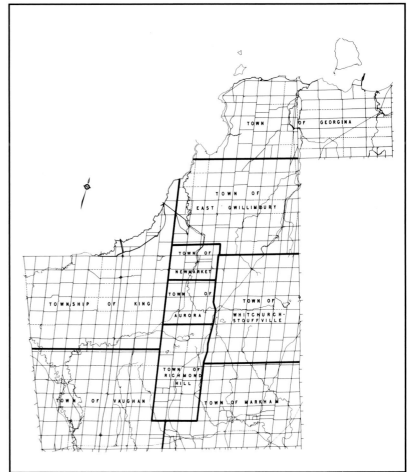

a mill, for example, other amenities such as a church, a school, a general store, and, later, a post office could eventually be found. The large number of hamlets in Whitchurch can perhaps be explained by the difficulties encountered in moving goods over a distance to and from the area in an era when both the means of transportation and the routes themselves left much to be desired.

As Whitchurch grew, so too did local government. In 1825 William Barber was appointed town clerk, and by the following year municipal organization included two wardens, an assessor, and a tax collector. These officials were Joseph Hewitt, town clerk; William Reader and J. Hewitt, assessors; Samuel Ball, collector; and Eli Gorham and John Bogart, Jr., town wardens. An 1836 act of the Legislative Assembly came into force to regulate municipal affairs. Under this act, commissioners replaced wardens, and the designation of township was used in place of town. Whitchurch's first commissioners were Samuel Pearson, Joshua Wilson, and Ludwick Wiedman.

By 1839 the term "warden" was once again in use; at this time, municipal affairs were conducted by a chairman and three wardens. The system was changed once again in 1850 with the implementation of the Baldwin Act. Under the provisions of this act, the Township of Whitchurch became an organized municipality with a reeve, deputy reeve, and three councillors. The reeve and deputy reeve also represented the township at York County Council. At the same time, counties replaced districts as the basic unit of local government organization. The inaugural meeting of the municipal government of the Township of Whitchurch was held at Smith's Inn in Stouffville on January 6, 1851. The reeve, Joseph Hartman, and councillors were appointed, not elected.

The Village of Newmarket was incorporated in 1858, and for this reason, was separated from Whitchurch for administrative purposes, as happened in the Village of Aurora in 1863, and Stouffville in 1877.

Boundary changes took place again after 1967 when the County of York requested a review of local government. This review resulted in a recommendation to establish a regional government that would help to minimize the disruption caused by rapid growth and economic development. On January 1, 1971, the County of York was dissolved and replaced by the Regional Municipality of York. Fourteen local municipalities existed before this change, but were consolidated into nine municipalities within the Region of York.

THE EXTERNAL BOUNDARIES of the new Region of York were unchanged from York County's. However, significant alterations were made in the boundaries of the municipalities. Whitchurch kept its northern and eastern boundaries (Davis Drive and Durham Road 30 respectively), but its western boundary was moved from Yonge Street to the then-proposed Highway 404, and its southern boundary moved farther south to four lots south of Stouffville/Gormley Sideroad. At the same time, Stouffville was added to the township, which was renamed the Town of Whitchurch-Stouffville.

CHAPTER 3

FROM PIT-SAW TO PINE PLANTATIONS

Early descriptions of the forest cover of Whitchurch Township are very meagre, but the seventeenth-century Jesuit missionaries described the highland forests as being predominately hard maple, either in pure stands or mixed with beech, cherry, oak, basswood, hemlock, and pine. These hardwood stands occurred on the more fertile soils, while pure stands of white pine or white and red pine were found on the lighter sandy soils. Cedar, black ash, elm, soft maple, and spruce occurred on the wet and moist sites. For the aboriginal people this was the forest that provided their hunting, trapping, and fishing areas and also supplied their recreation, food and shelter.

Prior to Euro-American settlement, the aboriginal and voyageur trails from Lake Ontario to Lake Simcoe, including the Humber route and the Rouge Trail through what was later to become Whitchurch Township, were through dense and trackless forests. The old Rouge Trail wound along the Rouge River, crossed the watershed via Vandorf, and then went north to what was later to become Newmarket, on the Holland River.

In 1794 Augustus Jones and the Queen's Rangers built Yonge Street to a site just north of present-day Thornhill. In 1794-95, William Berczy, later a renowned artist, built a wagon road from Thornhill to Holland Landing in exchange for land grants in Markham.

In 1804 another tortuous trail was carved out of the wilderness to carry settlers from Yonge Street by way of Vivian to Uxbridge. The old Stouffville Road, which in the 1830s and 1840s was still through largely unbroken forest, served mainly as a connecting link between York (Toronto) and Brock Township.

The Mast Road (approximately the tenth concession road) was developed from the pine ridge in Whitchurch Township, down the hog's back between the Big and Little Rouge rivers. Logs were teamed down this road by oxen drawing timber tugs (pairs of wheels supporting logs at each end). They were drawn to the Rouge, dumped into the river, and floated in rafts to Lake Ontario and then to Kingston and Quebec.

Many roads were built of 3-inch cedar or pine planks, and plank mills were established to provide this material. The plank roads were later gravelled over.

Before receiving patent for their land, settlers were required to clear for cultivation and fence ten acres, build a house 16 feet by 20 feet, and cut down all trees on the front of the lot. The pioneer regarded trees as his enemy and used fire and cattle to conquer them. Trees were felled with axes, cut into lengths, and hauled away to be burned. Brush was piled by hand and burnt, and cattle were used to browse down new growth.

It was not always the best land that was cleared first. The light sandy soils had more pine and were easier to clear. In addition, when the settlers saw the great pine trees, they thought the land had to be very fertile to grow such magnificent specimens. When they chopped them down, they found they had nothing but blowsand.

LOGGING AND SAWMILLING

IN THE EARLY 1800s special contractors to the Royal Navy were the only persons authorized to cut timber on Crown lands, although there was much illicit trade in the mast-and-spar industry, as well as in the square-timber trade, all of which boomed until about 1830.

Sawn lumber was first produced by Whitchurch settlers by means of a very primitive piece of equipment called a pit-saw. Pit-sawing required the digging of a pit or the erection of a framework. In both cases a man above and a man below pulled a saw up and down, and by this laborious method up to twenty-five boards could by sawn in a heavy day's work. This manual method evolved to a water wheel turning a crankshaft connected to a saw set vertically in the framework.

During the period 1800 to 1830 the little sawmills were important in helping the early settlers to clear the dense woods and in supplying lumber for local use. The settlers first used round or square logs to build their homes, then planks. Mills were owned by the community or operated on a shared basis, so boards were cut at little cost to the settler.

Sawmills not only formed the nucleus for a settlement but also provided employment for several sawyers, a blacksmith, and up to forty men involved in cutting and hauling timber. The development of a settlement generally followed a pattern: first, a simple and inexpensive sawmill, then a grist mill, a general store, a cooper's shop, a blacksmith's shop, a tavern, a tannery, a woollen mill, a distillery, and then a larger but still-primitive sawmill.

In addition to their importance in clearing the land for farming, these small sawmills were established because transportation was difficult, they could be built on small streams, and they could be constructed of cheap, readily available wood.

IN WHITCHURCH TOWNSHIP, beginning in the very early 1800s, small water-powered mills were established on the headwaters and tributary streams of the Rouge and the Holland rivers. Some of the sawmillers and the location of their mills are listed below.

Joseph Hill In 1801 Hill, one of Timothy Rogers's Quaker settlers, erected a sawmill on the Holland River on the east side of the dam on Water Street and just west of the railway tracks of present-day Newmarket. By 1805 it is recorded that settlers here were hard-pressed to get enough timber to build other mills.

John Bogart, Sr. In 1798 this Pennsylvania Quaker rode horseback from Pennsylvania to York County to look for land as well as mill sites. In 1802 his family made the 500-mile trek, bringing horses, oxen, "milch" cows, sheep, pigs, and poultry. They lived in a bark shelter at what was later to become Bogarttown until a log cabin could be built with two rooms, adzed basswood floors, and a chimney of mud and wattles. John Bogart dammed the Holland River and built a sawmill and grist mill in 1806.

Timothy Millard Millard erected a sawmill in the early 1800s at lot 94, concession 1.

George Lemon In 1805 Lemon received a grant of 200 acres on lot 8, concession 6. Two streams ran through his property. On the west stream he built a sawmill and on the east stream a grist mill. Seventy-five acres, including the sawmill, were separated from the Lemon properties in 1834.

Peter Brillinger Brillinger first came to the area in 1796. About 1802 he and his son, Peter, set up one of the first sawmills in Whitchurch Township on a tributary of the Rouge River, on lot 1, concession 4.

Simon Teal This Pennsylvania settler established one of the first sawmills in the township on lot 6, concession 4, on a branch of the Rouge River. This mill was abandoned in 1855.

Abraham Taylor Taylor operated a water-driven sawmill on the Holland River at the present location of Cedar Valley. This water-wheel mill was later owned and operated by Jesse Lundy.

Andrew Clubine Clubine opened a sawmill on lot 1, concession 5, just across the road from the Peter Brillinger sawmill.

Abraham Stouffer During the period from 1817 to 1824, Stouffer's mills, including a sawmill, flourished on the banks of the Rouge River in what is now the town of Stouffville.

Bruce's Mill In 1827 Casper Sherk located as a tenant on lot 34, concession 5 Markham, and by 1829-30, he had built a dam and a sawmill. He later built a grist mill and the sawmill was closed. A Mr. Dickson and a Mr. McNair ran the grist mill until about 1840.

THERE WERE UNDOUBTEDLY several other early sawmills operating from 1800 until about 1830, but during this period the local demand for lumber was very small and there was no convenient waterway to transport timber to the larger markets for square timber and masts or spars.

BOOM YEARS FROM 1850

PRIOR TO 1850 sawmills in counties along the north shore of Lake Ontario were generally small water-driven mills using local resources and were often intermixed with farming activity. All this changed and led to the establishment of many large steam or water-driven sawmills in Whitchurch Township during 1850-1900 for a number of interrelated reasons: the phenomenal growth of cities in the United States and the concomittant demand for sawn lumber; exhaustion of accessible stands of pine in the United States; a developing inland water transportation system that included canals and lake transport from such ports as Toronto and Port Hope to Oswego, New York; building of railroads through Whitchurch Township.

IN ADDITION the 1854 Reciprocity Treaty between Canada and the United States removed the duty from Canadian lumber exports, and the reservation of the King's white pine for mast

An early Whitchurch sawmill.
Whitchurch-Stouffville Museum

timber was temporarily lifted for approximately ten years (from 1870 to 1880). (Early land grants contained a White Pine Clause, which stated that white pine was reserved for the King, and fines of up to 50 pounds would be levied on anyone cutting down the potential masts or yard-arms.) The lumber trade in Whitchurch Township was profitable, but the boom did not last.

At the height of timbering, bogus settlers and illegal timber cutting added to the rapid destruction of the forest for square timber, masts and spars, lumber for the U.S. market, and fuel wood. By 1850 Whitchurch Township was only 35 per cent wooded and was further reduced to 7 per cent by 1910. In the 1990s forest cover in Whitchurch-Stouffville is approximately 22 per cent.

After 1850, and for the remainder of the nineteenth century, railways replaced sawmills as the major catalyst for the growth of towns and villages in the township and surrounding area. Railways allowed large volumes of local lumber to be transported to distant markets; their impact on Whitchurch Township was significant. The township was served by the Ontario,

Simcoe and Huron Railway, which arrived in Aurora 1853 (this became the Northern Railway in 1858); the Toronto and Nipissing Railway, built in 1871; the Lake Simcoe Junction Railway, built north from Stouffville through Ballantrae and Vivian in 1877; the Gormley, Vandorf, Pine Orchard line of the James Bay Railway, built in 1905.

During the 1870s railways monopolized the fuel wood trade from Whitchurch to Toronto, and the price paid to farmers for fuel wood was the same ($2.50 a cord) in 1880 as it was in 1870.

The number of sawmills started to decline by the 1880s. The best pine was gone and lumbermen took trees that would have been bypassed in earlier decades. About 1880 the government started claiming white pine for the Crown again. By the end of the century practically all the water sawmills were gone and only a few stationary steam mills remained. Small portable mills were still working, but lumbering was no longer a major activity in the township.

Just as the small sawmills were so important to the patterns of settlement and development of Whitchurch Township, the later mills and the booming lumbering business of the period from 1850 to 1900 were central to the economic and social life of many residents. For instance, the economic life of the hamlet of Ballantrae was sustained for many years by the four or five sawmills in that area. From the 1861 census, from the Upper Holland Conservation Authority Report, and from other sources, including maps, the following sawmills operated in Whitchurch during that hectic half century.

James Lloyd This water-driven mill was located on lot 78, concession 1, in what is now the southeast part of Aurora.

W.H. Cane After being burnt out twice in his Queensville location, William Cane reestablished a large steam sawmill and planing factory in Newmarket in 1874. Huge loads of logs, sometimes five hundred a day, were brought to this mill by two hundred or more teams owned by area farmers. Huron Street (now Davis Drive) as far as the eye could see was a long black line of loads of logs. Hauling logs was a lucrative business, and drivers sang and joked while the bells jingled and the sleigh runners squealed on the frozen snow.

Competitions were often held to determine who could haul the biggest load of logs. The heaviest load ever drawn to the Cane mill was hauled by Dr. James Hunter's team. It consisted of six green logs, measuring 2,728 board feet, with the total load weighing nearly 8 tons! Marvellous white pine 4 to 5 feet in diameter was cut to supply mills such as Cane's.

Alexander McKechnie This was a large steam mill listed in the 1861 census as employing six full-time male labourers and generating an annual value of product of $4,800. The mill was located on lot 68, concession 1, just northwest of Lake Willcocks in Oak Ridges.

John and Eugene Nash Dr. John Nash and his son, Eugene, operated this sawmill, in

conjunction with a grist mill, at the northeast corner of Huron (Davis Drive) and Main streets between the railway tracks and Main Street in Newmarket. These mills had been built in 1854 by Dr. Ford, but were burnt down in 1856. They were rebuilt about 1858.

Peter Brillinger, Sr.'s sawmill, lot 1, concession 4.
Whitchurch-Stouffville Museum

Daniel Williamson Williamson was a carpenter and builder by trade. He also owned and operated a steam sawmill just west of Preston Lake on lot 13, concession 3.

Jared Lloyd This was a water-driven mill located at the west side of the present-day Westview Golf Course at the intersection of Leslie Street (the third concession road) and the Vandorf Sideroad. It was on lot 15, concession 3, on the west branch of the Holland River. It was an integral part of the hamlet of White Rose, contributing to its development and prosperity.

Thomas Coates Coates operated a water-driven mill at the junction of present-day Leslie Street and St. John's Sideroad. It was located on lot 25, concession 3, and utilized water power provided by the west branch of the Holland River.

Peter Brillinger, Sr. Brillinger was one of the first settlers to establish a sawmill in Whitchurch. According to the census, he was still operating a "very good mill" in 1861. It was located on a headwater stream of the Rouge River on lot 1, concession 4.

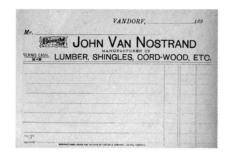

Peter Brillinger, Jr. The 1861 census entry for this mill indicates that Peter and George Brillinger were "operating a good mill and in good order" on this tributary of the Rouge River. The mill was located on lot 2, concession 4.

John Van Nostrand and George Harrison In 1854 Dr. James Hunter of Newmarket purchased part of lot 17, concession 4, and erected a small steam sawmill on 20 acres located on what was later known as the school creek (a branch of the Holland River). Dr. Hunter also purchased lot 15, concession 4, as a source of timber for the mill.

In 1855 John Van Nostrand and his brother-in-law George Harrison signed agreements to purchase all of lot 15 and the 20-acre parcel of lot 17 from Dr. Hunter. In 1856 they began what was to be a very important sawmill business. It was always in debt, both during the partnership and during the period from 1870 to 1895, after John Van Nostrand had purchased Harrison's interest in 1870, owing to continued expansion of the business and purchase of timber lots to the north and east of the village.

This industry established the village of Vandorf, called Van Nostrand's Mills for many years, and provided employment and accommodation for many mill workers. In the 1861 census the operation is described as a "splendid steam unit and owners George Harrison and John Van Nostrand are doing a good business."

The mill had a large elevated track to transport logs into the mill as well as its own blacksmith's shop, which was destroyed by fire in 1870. By 1885 the mill was sawing approximately 1,000,000 feet of lumber a year, most of which was teamed to Aurora and shipped by rail to destinations in Canada and the United States.

It is interesting to note that insurance data from the Van Nostrand account journals for 1880 indicate that the fire-insurance premium was $25 a year when the mill was idle and 60 cents a month for each $100 of coverage when the mill was operating, for a total coverage of $1,000. Notice was given to the agent and the

Van Nostrand family collection

insurance company that in 1880 the mill would operate only in the months of April, May, and June.

    John Van Nostrand died in 1895, and the mill operated for only a few years after his death.

Richard and Thomas Lewis The Richard Lewis mill operation at lot 5, concession 1, was carried on in four different buildings, two of them latterly destroyed by fire. The 1861 census enumerator described the Lewis operation as a "good mill and in very good order." It is interesting to note that ten men operated this mill during the one-hundred-year period of its existence from the 1840s to the 1940s. They were Richard Lewis, Thomas Lewis, George Laing, Joseph Leary, Jacob Heise, Joseph Collard, Sam Doner, Mr. Lageer, Frank Harvey, and Joseph Sider.

John Van Nostrand sawmill, Vandorf.
Whitchurch-Stouffville Museum

Dr. James Hunter Hunter sold his steam mill at Vandorf to Harrison and Van Nostrand in 1855. He was reeve of Newmarket in 1859, and in 1869 he was operating a sawmill on the east part of lot 16, concession 5. He owned several timber lots in the area of this mill and, about 1871, sold the west 155 acres of lot 16, concession 5 to Thomas Lewis. Lewis sold almost immediately to John Van Nostrand, who in turn sold it to W. D. Richardson in 1907. Richardson established a sawmill on Vandorf Creek and sawed the pine, cedar, and hardwood on the lot.

Edward Randall This Pine Orchard mill located on lot 30, concession 5, was one of the larger mills that had been built about 1840 to meet the growing demand for lumber resulting from increased development around Lake Simcoe.

George Richardson David Richardson (George's father) purchased lot 25, concession 6, in the early days of settlement, and George operated the mill for four years, beginning in 1869. He had considerable previous sawmilling experience, having worked at the large Van Nostrand mill at Vandorf. The sawmill was in an area that became known as Seldom Seen, a term coined by George Richardson to describe the place's isolation in the 1860s.

Robert McCormick The 1861 census indicates that McCormick operated a sawmill at lot 29, concession 7, in partnership with Robert Hasty and James Simpson. McCormick had many timber lots in the pine area of Whitchurch Township and was a major influence in the village of Vivian, where he had a large sawmill, a general store, and a large residence. He prospered during the lumbering boom from 1860 to 1895 and employed hundreds of men in the woods and in his large steam mill located southwest of Vivian, adjacent to the Lake Simcoe Junction Railway. His involvement in cutting, hauling, and milling thousands of the giant white and red pine stems growing in the Whitchurch sands made him a major player in the economic, social, and cultural life of northeast Whitchurch.

Charles Appleton Appleton's mill was on the west side of Musselman's Lake on lot 18, concession 8. The lake was a source of water for his steam-powered sawmill.

John Bartholomew This water-driven mill, located on lot 3, concession 9, just north of present-day Millard Street in the Town of Stouffville, was in use during the 1850s and '60s. It was established in 1852 by Philip Bartholomew and was operated in later years by Lewis, John, and Aubrie Bartholomew.

Frederick Johnson Johnson's sawmill was on the northwest side of Island Lake in lot 20, concession 9. The lake was a source of water for the steam-driven sawmill, which utilized the huge pine resources of that area.

OTHER MILLS on the tributaries of the Rouge River were operated by Israel Clubine (lot 1, concession 5), Samuel Dick (concession 5), John and Isaac Gordon (concession 5), Phillip Cook (lot 1, concession 6), John Burkholder (lot 4, concession 6), John Baker (lot 9, concession 8), A. Sangster (lot 8, concession 9). Mills in the northern half of the township were operated by Abraham Taylor (lot 30, concession 6) and Arthur Stapleton (lot 22, concession 9).

Robert McCormick mill, Vivian.
Whitchurch-Stouffville Museum

← taken 1870's

William Ratcliff, Jr., eldest son of Ratcliff Mills founder.
Whitchurch-Stouffville Museum

FACING PAGE, ABOVE: *Abandoned farm, Vivian area.* Ministry of Natural Resources

BELOW: *View of a typical eroding gulley, 1951.* Ministry of Natural Resources

The Ratcliff Mill, just outside the boundaries of nineteenth-century Whitchurch Township, had a significant impact on the lumbering and the settlement of the township.

William Ratcliff Ratcliff, a native of England, arrived in Markham Township in 1851, after spending a few years in Rochester, N.Y., and in Pickering Township. He had farmed in England and wasted no time building a sawmill on lot 3, concession 6, on the Rouge River. This mill was fully operational by 1852 and Ratcliff's enterprise flourished. In addition to strong local demand for mill products from prosperous wheat farmers who were building new homes, the export trade to the United States flourished because of the Reciprocity Treaty.

The water power for this mill was supplied by a 3-acre mill pond at the head of the Little Rouge River. In 1900 its natural level was increased by the flow of water from six artesian wells drilled just north of the mill. The mill's two water wheels (one to power the machinery and one to provide electricity) were replaced by a diesel engine in 1936. In the early days the saw was one of the old up-and-down types, but in the 1880s it was replaced by circular saws up to 5 feet in diameter.

The mill operation, started in 1851, continues today via retail lumber outlets at Unionville and Gormley. Successive generations of Ratcliffs have operated this unique enterprise for more than 140 years. It not only has utilized thousands of board feet of the fine Whitchurch white pine, but also many thousands of feet of hardwoods. Many of the Ratcliff timber lots were in Whitchurch Township, and the Ratcliffs purchased hundreds of loads of logs from settlers and farmers north of their mill. The Ratcliff sawmill and lumber business were major influences on the settlement, growth, and development of Whitchurch.

RETURN OF THE TREES

AS A RESULT OF THE HEAVY TIMBERING ACTIVITY and intensive cultivation for agriculture, large areas of wasteland were created in the light sandy soils of Whitchurch Township and many other areas of southern Ontario. Initially the pine was used to build homesteads, huge volumes were sold as square timber to Britain, and later, even larger quantities were shipped as lumber to the United States. Large volumes of hardwood were piled and burned to make potash, and after a few decades of farming, the light sandy areas were farmed out.

In the 1890s and after the turn of the century, the open fields became blowsand deserts, drifting sands blocked many roads, the split rail fences were soon buried, and on dry windy days the Whitchurch sky was yellow from blowing sand. Farmers jokingly referred to "shifting deeds," since soil from one farm would end up across the road on another's property.

In the hilly areas of the pine ridge, water erosion also played havoc with the light soils, washing away nutrient-rich topsoil and causing great gullies on the barren hillsides and along the watercourses of the Holland and the Rouge headwaters.

The Rouge, the Don, and Holland watershed areas lost their ability to act as water-storage areas, and many Whitchurch communities suffered from severe flooding in the spring and disastrous drought during the summer.

Between 1870 and 1900 there was a growing concern about the loss of agricultural productivity and the thousands of acres of wasteland developing in southern Ontario. During the 1870s farmers were encouraged to plant trees along roads and highways, and many of the old roadside maple trees in the Whitchurch area result from this early planting program; municipalities encouraged such roadside reforestation by paying landowners 25 cents a tree.

Blowsand left roots exposed on pine stumps.
Ministry of Natural Resources

Farmers, fruit growers, and many others were concerned about the lack of trees and forests, and in 1902 the Forestry Committee of the Ontario Agricultural and Experimental Union sent a resolution to the provincial government urging immediate action on the reforestation of wastelands in "Old Ontario." This action finally took place largely through the efforts of E.C. Drury, premier of Ontario in 1919, and E.J. Zavitz, forestry lecturer at Guelph and later provincial forester. Zavitz (considered to be the Father of Reforestation in Ontario) and Drury (who farmed at Crown Hill in Simcoe County) toured many of the barren wastelands with a horse and buggy during the period from 1905 to 1908.

After Zavitz completed a major study and submitted a very detailed report on the need for reforestation and forest management, the Counties Reforestation Act was passed in 1911, followed by the Reforestation Act in 1921. This 1921 legislation provided for the establishment of tree nurseries and the provision of tree seedlings as well as planting and management by the province. Counties were empowered to purchase barren farmland, often from tax sales, and put it under "management agreement" with the Ministry of Lands and Forests.

In "Old Ontario," the main areas of concern included the sand plains of Simcoe County and the barren hillsides of what is now the Oak Ridges moraine, running through York, Ontario, Durham, and Northumberland counties. Simcoe County led the way by signing the first Forestry Agreement in 1922, followed by York County (and others) in 1924.

In York County, reforestation action for the Whitchurch wastelands was initiated by county and township officials. George Pajet chaired the reforestation committee, and a management agreement with the province led to the purchase of the Hollidge property and planting of the first tree seedling in Vivian Forest in 1924.

Erosion destroyed this Whitchurch farmland, 1951.
Ministry of Natural Resources

During 1924 an additional 400 acres were purchased in Whitchurch and subsequent additional purchases increased the Vivian Forest area to 1,166 acres by 1938 and to 4,900 acres by 1983. A large portion of York Regional Forest is situated in Whitchurch Township.

It seems appropriate that reclamation of the blowing sand should have begun in the Vivian-Ballantrae area, where cutting down the pine forest and intensive agricultural use of the sandy soils had created the barren wasteland. Morgan Baker, M.P.P. York North, and Major "Lex"

West main tract, Vivian, part of the agreement forest properties, 1958.
Ministry of Natural Resources

McKenzie, M.P.P. York North, were very supportive of the tree-planting program and the "agreement forest" scheme for the Whitchurch properties. Morgan Baker, also reeve of Whitchurch Township for several years and chairman of the reforestation committee, was able to lead the conservation crusade to hold the blowing sand and rehabilitate the eroded farms. Other municipal officials who were members of the reforestation committee in 1924 included W.G. Scarace, W.G. Cohn, P.W. Pearson, and R. Marshall.

These far-sighted municipal officials and provincial politicians worked closely in a co-operative spirit with dedicated provincial foresters and local staff. The 197-acre Hollidge farm (lot 28, concession 8) was the first purchase for Vivian Forest. Part of the deal required that Ted Hollidge be the first caretaker for the forest. The Hollidge houses and barn were used as the first field office, and the Hollidge barn is still an integral part of the present-day Vivian Forest headquarters.

Scots pine, red pine, jack pine, Carolina poplar, European larch, and white spruce were some of the tree species planted in the blowsand pockets and in shallow furrows made by single-furrow ploughs pulled by horses through the sandy, eroding fields. Plantations were protected from fire, insects, and disease and were thinned and crop-tree pruned at appropriate intervals. Any natural hardwood areas on the agreement forest properties were rehabilitated through protection, selection improvement, and harvest cuts.

As a result productive plantations and woodlots have now replaced the eroding topsoil and barren sandy deserts of the Whitchurch wastelands. Such properties now yield a significant volume of forest products and are increasingly used for outdoor recreation and forest education. Much of the area has been returned to its former forested state, so water- and soil-holding capacities have improved significantly, spring flooding and summer drought have been reduced, and water storage in the headwaters of the Rouge and Holland watersheds has been ameliorated.

Whitchurch Township was one of the cradles for the co-operative municipal agreement forest program. Many private landowners in the area have also returned trees to poor sandy farms, either in Christmas-tree operations or in long-term timber-production plantings.

Windbreaks have been planted, and many private woodlots have been soundly managed and improved. Nevertheless, Whitchurch-Stouffville residents must ever be vigilant to treat trees and forests with respect if they wish to continue enjoying the many economic and environmental benefits provided by the area's woodlands.

Pine forests and lumbering were an integral part of settlement and development in Whitchurch, creating much of the wealth and social fabric of its pioneer communities. Excesses and carelessness led to blowsand and erosion by the beginning of this century. In the 1990s care must be taken so that urbanization and concrete road-building do not repeat the destruction to our forest heritage.

CHAPTER 4

THE COMMUNITIES OF WHITCHURCH

Settlers arriving in Whitchurch at the beginning of the nineteenth century lost no time in establishing services to satisfy their needs. John Bogart and his brother Martin took up land in what would become Bogarttown in 1803. By 1805 John had built his sawmill, and by 1806 his grist mill was in operation. Similarly Abraham Stouffer, having arrived in 1804, was operating a grist mill in present-day Stouffville by 1817. As the century progressed, stores, post offices, hotels, and a variety of artisans' shops grew up around these services providing the communities with their necessities.

Poorly cleared and maintained roads made travel difficult in the early years of settlement, and small villages grew up at numerous crossroads to serve the neighbourhood. Often consisting of little more than a general store and post office, a church, and perhaps a mill or blacksmith's shop, these hamlets frequently disappeared as travel to larger centres became easier. The routes that the railways followed determined which of the centres would grow into towns and which would fail.

The three largest towns in the original Township of Whitchurch eventually incorporated and separated politically from the township. Aurora, incorporated in 1863, and Newmarket, in 1858, have not only remained apart from the Township of Whitchurch, but over the years have expanded to include portions of Whitchurch Township. Since the history of both Aurora and Newmarket is included in other publications, this book is concerned with the two towns only until the date of their incorporation.

Stouffville, incorporated in 1877, remained politically separate from Whitchurch until 1971, when the Regional Municipality of York was created. It then rejoined the township as the largest community in the Town of Whitchurch-Stouffville. Because the history of the village and the township are closely intertwined, the book follows the history of the town of Stouffville throughout its development.

Many of the crossroad villages have disappeared, their locations now evident only on community road signs. As the prosperity of these hamlets fluctuated greatly, often depending on a single business, their histories are difficult to trace. Although some communities have been well documented by local historians, others are remembered by little other than their

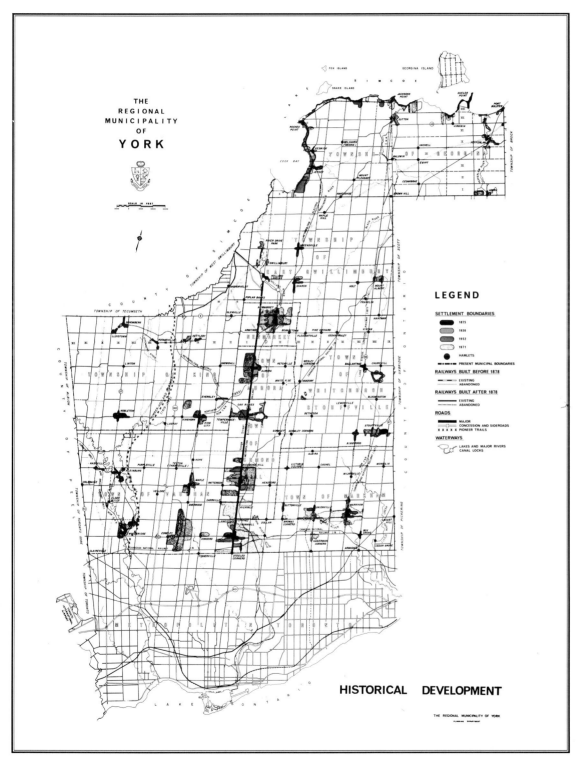

Historical development
The Regional Municipality of
York

names. For this reason, the community histories that follow differ greatly in length and detail. Where it has been possible, founding families have been identified for each community, along with the origin of the community's name. We have not been able to include accounts of all those persons who together created present-day Whitchurch-Stouffville; space permits us to highlight one or two whose legacy has been unique. The list of Sources and the Bibliography should help readers wishing to pursue further research.

OAK RIDGES, BOND LAKE, WILCOX LAKE, FRENCH SETTLEMENT

Oak Ridges, Bond Lake, Wilcox Lake, French Settlement
Lynne Rubbens

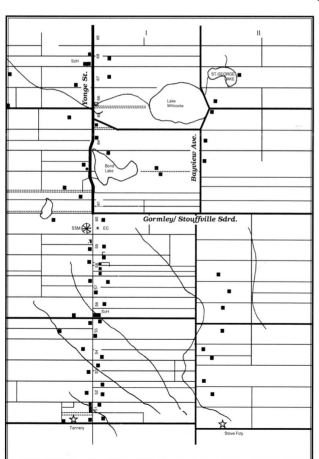

The part of Whitchurch Township south of Aurora, bordered by Yonge Street and the Gormley/Stouffville Sideroad, takes in the eastern section of Oak Ridges, and Wilcox Lake (originally Lake Willcocks), Lake St. George, and Bond Lake.

The history of Oak Ridges and the Bond Lake area can be traced back to the French Revolution, which began in 1789.

A number of royalists, supporters of Louis XIV, fled France for Britain after the monarch was deposed. The British government proposed that the émigrés be granted free land in Upper Canada. Lieutenant-Governor Simcoe was directed to select an area for the French settlers, and he chose lots 51 to 61 on both sides of Yonge Street. This uninhabited area was chosen partly because it was felt that York (Toronto) was vulnerable to a surprise aboriginal attack. A French settlement north of York would provide a protective shield for the southern areas.

About forty settlers arrived in Kingston in 1798 with the Comte de Puisaye, who was in charge of the group, consisting of aristocrats, fifteen soldiers, and eleven servants.

The town site was named Windham in honour of the member of the British Parliament responsible for the immigration of the de Puisaye settlers to Upper Canada. The area was surveyed in 1799, and workers began to clear the bush and build houses. Soon eighteen houses, a church, and a parsonage were completed.

With their aristocratic background, the settlers were ill equipped to deal with life at Windham, and the settlement was abandoned by 1806.

Laurent Quetton St. George was the sole member of the group to take advantage of the opportunities of his new home. He acquired considerable land through grants and speculation as a real estate agent. He began a fur trade with the native people and provided settlers with dry goods, groceries, and hardware. St. George both exported furs to and imported goods from New York and England.

When the monarchy was restored in 1815, St. George returned to France. He died there in 1821 without ever returning to Upper Canada, where he had amassed 26,000 acres.

Laurent Quetton St. George owned land on Yonge Street but not around Lake St. George. This land was originally owned by William Bond. Bond acquired lots 7 and 8, concession 2, in 1798, adding to his holdings around Bond Lake.

By 1799 he had constructed a log house on lot 64, concession 1 (Yonge Street). Bond quickly sold lots 7 and 8, concession 2 (Lake St. George), to William Willcocks in 1798. Like Bond, Willcocks did not live at the lake property.

Oak Ridges developed on the east and west sides of Yonge Street, making it part of both Whitchurch (east) and King (west) townships. In 1793, Lieutenant-Governor Simcoe ordered Yonge Street to be opened north to Holland Landing, but as late as 1801 Yonge Street was still practically impassable beyond Eglinton Avenue. It was, however, used as a transportation route by the North-West Fur Company. By 1832 conditions had improved enough to allow several stagecoaches to travel up Yonge Street, connecting York with steamers at Holland Landing, and so to Lake Simcoe via the Holland River. In the late 1830s toll gates were placed on Yonge Street to raise money for road improvements. Oak Ridges was south of the fifth toll gate, constructed at the present site of the Aurora cemetery.

First settlers in the Oak Ridges area included James Whitney at lot 66 on Yonge Street, Charles Fathers, Frederick Smith, and Capt. William Graham.

Gradually the Oak Ridges community developed. The Bond Lake Hotel, on the west side of the lake, was erected in 1834, and had more than twenty rooms, a ballroom, and a tavern. It was a favourite destination of sleigh parties from the surrounding areas and was frequented by curlers who played on the lake. The hotel operated until about 1902. The first post office in Oak Ridges, opened in 1851, was at lot 68, concession 1, in a general store built in 1846 by William Chadwick and subsequently owned by Alexander McKechnie, the postmaster. In 1857 Oak Ridges had a blacksmith's shop operated by the Routledge family and in 1867 a sawmill run by Thomas Gregory. The oldest church in Oak Ridges is the Anglican St. John the Baptist, constructed in 1848.

The first Oak Ridges school, opened in 1854, was a union school, serving students from two townships, (U.S.S. #1) with King Township taking in all children east and west of Yonge Street. It was located at lot 68, concession 1, King, on land that had been owned by W. Wilcox Baldwin. The present elementary school was built on the same site in 1914, with a gymnasium addition in 1961.

Henri Quetton St. George, son of Laurent, came to Canada with his family in 1847. Henri purchased parts of lots 6, 7 and 8, concession 2, around Lake St. George, between 1852 and 1860. The property was known as Glen Lonely, and Henri constructed a château, described as a four-storey mansion with beautiful lawns, gardens, barns, stables, and breeding stock. Henri was the first owner to actually live at Lake St. George. He inhabited his château until his death in 1896. The building was destroyed by fire in 1906.

Original lease for the Bond Lake Hotel, 1885.

Dibb family collection

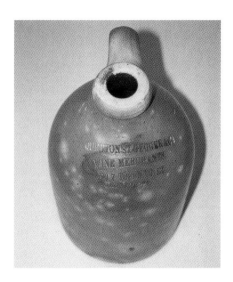

Advertising jug from Quetton St. George & Co. Wine Merchants, owned by Henri Quetton St. George.
Markham District Historical Museum

Many Upper Canadian politicians and prominent people had country estates at Oak Ridges. These included the Baldwins, the Boultons, the McLeods, and the Irwins.

In 1898 the William Bond property at Bond Lake was sold to the Metropolitan Railway. The railway converted the farm into a public park, which became a popular spot for picnics, baseball games, boating, and swimming. The radial line of the Metropolitan Railway ran alongside this park, which became a favourite stopping point for travellers both winter and summer. The Bond Lake park was closed to the public in 1928, and the radial line discontinued in 1930. The Bond Lake Tavern was frequented by sleigh parties from the surrounding area. The lake area also provided timber resources, which were felled and milled at a Yonge Street sawmill operated by the Mortson family.

About 1900 Oak Ridges had two main industries: a brickyard was located at Lake Willcocks (Wilcox Lake), and the Lake Simcoe Ice and Fuel company, which cut lake ice for sale.

Many of the seasonal Wilcox Lake residences became year-round homes after the Second World War, when housing was very scarce. An increase in the school population meant that Wilcox Lake needed its own school. One was constructed in 1951, with an addition in 1955. The original building burnt down in 1971, and a third section, built later that year, is still in use as the Lake Wilcox Public School.

The Oak Ridges, Bond Lake, and Wilcox Lake areas remained part of the Township of Whitchurch until the creation of the Regional Municipality of York in 1971, when they became part of the Town of Richmond Hill.

WILCOX LAKE AT E

Wilcox Lake
Whitchurch-Stouffville Museum

H.E.P.C. radial cars at Bond Lake,
about to leave for Toronto.
Aurora Museum

Bond Lake property owned by John
Beverly Robinson.
Whitchurch-Stouffville Museum

AURORA

ABOVE:: Trinity Anglican Church, built 1846.

BELOW LEFT: Doan Hall, Yonge Street, built 1855, demolished 1969.

BELOW RIGHT: Charles Doan's first house and post office, Yonge Street and Catherine Avenue, built early 1800s, demolished 1982.

Aurora Museum

When Lieutenant-Governor Simcoe gave his orders for the construction of the road north from the capital at York to the Holland Landing, it was to be a military road to provide access to the fort at Penetanguishene on Georgian Bay a safe distance from the American border because the threat of war between the Americans and British was a constant concern. The trail was blazed in 1793, marked the following year, and completed in 1796. Often impassable, the road was named Yonge Street in honour of Sir George Yonge, British secretary of state for war. The road was used only briefly for military purposes but provided the main route for settlement north from York. It would also form the boundary dividing Aurora between the Township of King on the west side and the Township of Whitchurch on the east.

The construction of the first known building in Aurora coincided with the development of Yonge Street. Situated on a rise at the northeast corner of the present Yonge Street and Catherine Avenue, the saltbox-style house stood until 1982, when it was demolished. In the early 1800s Charles Doan occupied this house and operated the first post office from there. Catherine Avenue, which bordered the house on the south, was named for Charles's second wife.

Until 1805, settlement was distributed along Yonge Street on 200-acre parcels. By 1805 lots 76 to 83 on the west (King) side of Yonge and lots 78 to 83 on the east (Whitchurch) side had been deeded by the Crown to various settlers, and these properties form almost all present-day Aurora. The legacy of several early settlers is street names in the old part of town: streets running through their original Crown grants bear the names of William Tyler and William Kennedy and his son Reuben. Charles and Robert Irwin operated a grist mill on the

creek just west of Yonge Street and gave their name to Irwin Avenue, Machell Street is a reminder of an early general merchant, Richard Machell (opened his store in 1834), and of Aurora's first name, Machell's Corners.

The tiny community grew slowly around the crossroads. By 1825 most of the original lots were still intact. In 1818 William Tyler gave a corner of his property for a Methodist church, and the United church remains on the corner to this day. The earliest hotel, McLeod's, at the north end of town, played a part in the Rebellion of 1837. Several prominent citizens were active in the rebellion, including Charles Doan, who was jailed for five months for his part. Not all Aurora citizens were sympathetic to William Lyon Mackenzie's rebels, however. James Mosley, a Loyalist, actually warned the government that the rebels were on the march.

The first post office in Whitchurch opened in Charles Doan's home in July 1846, with Doan as first postmaster.

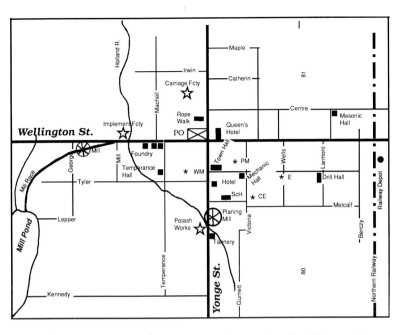

ABOVE: *Aurora, based on* Illustrated Historical Atlas of County of York, *1878.* Lynne Rubbens BELOW: *The Aurora Agricultural Works, established 1859, makers of the Fleury plough.* Aurora Museum

It operated from this location for a number of years until Doan opened a new store on the northwest corner of Wellington and Yonge streets. Shortly thereafter he built an imposing new home, Doan Hall, just north of his store. In 1854 the flourishing town was in need of a new name and Doan chose Aurora, the goddess of the dawn, to symbolize the dawning of a new age for the settlement that was experiencing tremendous growth following the opening of the Ontario, Simcoe and Huron Railway the previous year.

On May 16, 1853, the first train to operate in Canada West arrived in Aurora, marking the beginning of a new era. The town grew quickly, with new hotels springing up along Wellington Street East near the station and new industries being created by the transportation facilities. In 1859 the Aurora Agricultural Works opened its foundry on Wellington Street West, providing employment for much of Aurora's populace for over three-quarters of a century. The Fleury plough, named for the founder of the business, was the basis for an industry that employed more than two hundred men in its heyday. Other businesses, many associated with the foundry, opened over the next few years. Millers, carriage makers, a rope walk, (a long, covered building where rope was manufactured), a brewery, a cooperage, and potash works were all operating within a few years of the coming of rail transportation.

Cultural pursuits kept pace with industrial progress. In 1856 the Mechanics Institute was founded and soon opened a library for the use of the public. Education was organized circa 1822, and about 1840 the first school opened on the west side of Yonge Street, north of Kennedy Street. When the Methodists built their new frame church in 1855, they moved the old log one to the back of the property and used it for a schoolhouse. In 1857 a brick school was built on the north side of Church Street to attend to the needs of the growing community. The first Anglican church was built in 1846, and a New Connexion Methodist church stood

ABOVE: Yonge Street, Aurora, looking north. Picture taken in 1870s.
BELOW: New Connexion Methodist Church, Mosley Street, built 1856-57.
Aurora Museum

on Mosley Street. The town also boasted a Temperance Hall and a Rising Sun Masonic Hall.

By 1863 the village had been growing steadily for a decade, and the decision was made to incorporate to allow the village to elect its own municipal council and separate it from both the townships of Whitchurch and King. The first reeve of Aurora was Charles Doan, who, with Seth Ashton, Robert Boyd, James Holliday, and George Stevenson, presided over the affairs of the town. One of their first responsibilities was to choose a design for the town crest; their selection shows the rising sun over the hills of Whitchurch with the Fleury plough. The village continued to prosper, with fine new homes and industries being built, many of which still stand within the town's historic core.

The Toronto. *This engine, built for the Ontario, Simcoe and Huron Railroad Union Company (later the Northern Railway Company of Canada), was the first locomotive built in Canada. It was manufactured by James Good of Toronto in May 1853. On May 16, 1853, the locomotive headed the first train leaving Toronto. The train, consisting of four yellow-painted coaches, went to Machell's Corners, which is now Aurora.*
Public Archives

NEWMARKET

Timothy Rogers, a Quaker and United Empire Loyalist, was responsible for bringing the first settlers from the eastern United States to Newmarket. In 1801 forty 200-acre lots were assigned to him for settlement by himself and other Quaker families. More Quakers soon followed to the area, settling in Newmarket as well as Schomberg, Sharon, Pine Orchard, Uxbridge, Bogarttown, and Pickering.

Two of the original settlers helped create the centre of business and commerce in Newmarket. Joseph Hill erected the first mill and dam on the west bank of the river at the south side of today's Water Street. James Kinsey, the miller, began to grind wheat before the end of 1801. Nearby, Hill built a store, and to the west, near today's Presbyterian church, a wooden residence. South of this first mill, on the northeast corner of lot 92, concession 1, Elisha Beman built a second mill about 1803. This mill was the start of Beman's move to gain control of many of the commercial operations in the fledgling community. In 1804 Beman purchased the rights to the Hill mill and store, and by 1805 he had bought enough land to control the intersection of present-day Main Street and the mill.

Beman extended a road from the mill to Yonge Street, now Eagle Street. His road provided a permanent link to York. He then gained control of lot 33, concession 2, where Joseph Hill had illegally constructed a tannery on Crown land. Eventually Hill also lost his sawmill, constructed opposite the grist mill, to Peter Robinson, Elisha Beman's stepson. By 1812 the Beman-Robinson family was highly influential in both Newmarket and the fur trade.

Eli Gorham set up four carding machines in Joseph Hill's grist mill in 1809; this was reputedly the first such machinery brought to Upper Canada for manufacture of woollen goods. Gorham's own mill, dam, and factory were erected in 1811 on the stream to the south of today's Gorham Street. By 1841 the woollen mill had been enlarged, relocated to the north side of Gorham, and employed thirty men. The mills manufactured flannels, satinettes, wool blankets, and provided a market to which farmers could bring fleece.

In 1814 William Roe entered into partnership with Andrew Borland to trade with native people in the area. By 1820 three stores were located in Newmarket. The fur trade provided a market for native people other than that at York on Lake Ontario. The fur trade reached its peak about 1825, and

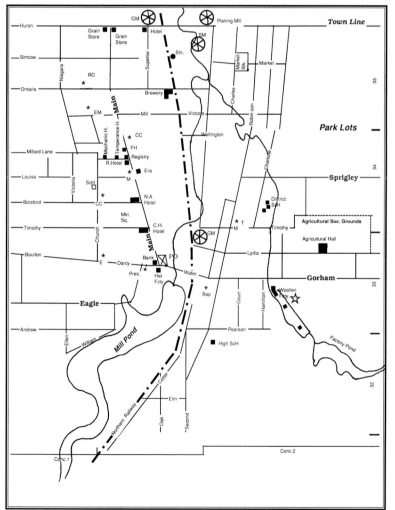

Newmarket, based on Illustrated Historical Atlas of County of York, *1878.* Lynne Rubbens

each spring saw three hundred to four hundred aboriginal people arriving in Newmarket to trade. As the importance of the fur trade waned, milling and other commercial activities became more important.

The first tavern in Newmarket was established on Eagle Street. It is not known when it opened, but it was in operation by 1819. The second public house was opened about 1820 on the southwest corner of Main and Botsford streets, where the present King George Hotel stands. Other early hotels in the town included the North American, built in 1826 on Main Street, and the Mansion House, also on Main Street and built before 1837.

Important amenities for the town continued to develop. Newmarket's first post office was established in 1822. W.B. Robinson was the first postmaster, serving until 1837. He was followed by William Roe, who held the job until his death in 1879. A stagecoach line connected Newmarket with other communities in 1825.

The Quakers, many of whom settled on Yonge Street, were granted a preparative meeting in 1804 by the Pelham monthly meeting in the Niagara area, so the group of Quakers had been established or sanctioned as a local community meeting, or congregation (see Appendix A). The local meeting reported to the monthly meeting, which in turn reported to the yearly meeting in Philadelphia. In 1806 Newmarket was established as a monthly meeting, and Whitchurch Quakers who met at Pine Orchard became a preparative meeting to Newmarket. Their meeting house, erected in 1810 at lot 92, concession 1 west, on Yonge Street, still stands and is used by Quakers today.

NEWMARKET, Ont.   Looking Northwest.

Main Street, Newmarket, Ont. Canada.

ABOVE: View to northwest across Fairy Lake. BELOW: View to north along Main Street, circa early 1890s.
Whitchurch-Stouffville Museum

Main Street, Newmarket, c. 1874
Newmarket Historical Society

The first church in the main part of Newmarket was built by the Episcopal Methodists at the northeast corner of Prospect and Timothy streets in 1824. All denominations in town were welcome to the building when it was not in use by the Methodists. It was torn down in 1883.

The Christian denomination originated in the United States in 1804 and came to Canada in 1810, when a congregation was formed in Charlottetown. A church was established in Keswick, Ontario, in 1821. Newmarket's Christian church began to organize in 1822. A permanent church, on Main Street, was not built until 1874.

Other churches were constructed in subsequent years. By 1845 these included Anglican, Presbyterian, Congregational, and Roman Catholic.

The first school in Newmarket was established by the Society of Friends (Quakers), although it was open to non-Quakers as well. Prior to the construction of the Yonge Street

Meeting House, classes were held in various homes. A permanent public school was not established until 1824. In 1824 Robert Srigley deeded a portion of lot 12, concession 2 (present-day Prospect Street), for a school, and in succeeding years classes were conducted in various places on this site. The Alexander Muir School was the last building actually constructed for a school. It was used until 1976 and demolished in 1979.

A union school with King Township, known as the Armitage School (U.S.S. #3), was built on lot 88, concession 1, fronting on Yonge Street. The actual date of construction is not known, but the school was included on the 1860 Tremaine Map of York County. In 1969–70 the Armitage School was closed and the building was used as the head office of the York Region Real Estate Board. In 1990 the building was demolished when the surrounding property was developed.

Newmarket continued to evolve as a trading centre for the surrounding area. In 1853 the Ontario, Simcoe and Huron Railway reached Newmarket from Toronto, thus encouraging the growth and development of Newmarket at the expense of other surrounding communities, such as Bogarttown.

On January 1, 1858, Newmarket was separated from the Township of Whitchurch and incorporated as a municipality. Municipal elections were held January 4 and 5, 1858, and the first reeve was Donald Sutherland; councillors were William Roe, Erastus Jackson, George H. Bache, William Wallis, and the clerk was Edwin Penrose Irwin.

*ABOVE: **St. Paul's Church of England, Newmarket.** Whitchurch-Stouffville Museum*
*BELOW: **View of Yonge Street at Armitage along Metropolitan Railway Line, 1924.** Aurora Museum*

WHITE ROSE

Jared Lloyd's grist mill and the renowned White Rose flour that he produced gave the name to this rural community. A fast-flowing stream on the southeast corner of Leslie Street (the third concession road) and the Vandorf Sideroad (lot 15, concession 3) provided the water power for both the grist mill and a sawmill in the mid-1800s. The Lloyd family founded and operated these mills, along with the post office, which opened in 1863 in the mill office. Jared Lloyd served as postmaster from 1864 to 1887.

By 1886 the flour mill was operated by steam power, the dam having been washed out repeatedly during spring floods. Millers included Matthew Love, who had purchased lot 16, concession 3 in 1870, and his sons, Moses and Enoch (who married Emma Lloyd, Jared's daughter). The mill was sold and torn down in 1903, and nothing remains but the stone foundation. The water wheel is reported to have been moved to Cedar Valley about 1905.

A general store on lot 12, concession 3, served the White Rose community from 1869, when John Richardson was the storekeeper. Others ran a store at the same location from 1887 to 1899. From 1906 to 1912 the store was closed, then reopened under William Woodcock and operated for a further year and a half.

A small hall on the northeast corner of the Vandorf Sideroad and Leslie Street was erected by the Sons of Temperance and used for community functions. It was leased to Stephen Wallace by the owner of lot 16, Matthew Love.

Several White Rose residents were patrons of the 1878 *Illustrated Historical Atlas of the County of York.* Matthew Love, living on lot 17, concession 3, was a miller, and William Scott (lot 10, concession 3), Stephen Wallace (lot 15, concession 2), and G.W. Graham (lot 18, concession 3) were listed as farmers. George Lloyd was listed as a wagonmaker.

After the closing of the White Rose Flour Mills, the area reverted to primarily agricultural use. In 1914 the post office also closed. Little remains today of the bustling mill site that gave this community its name.

Until 1870 Wesleyan Methodists worshipped in a small log church and a Primitive Methodist church stood just north of S.S. #6 school on lot 10, concession 3. This parcel of land had been deeded to the church trustees in 1856 by Henry and Alice Painter and was retained by the trustees until 1894, when it was sold. The building was demolished in 1884.

In June 1870 Mark and Charity Steele deeded a portion of lots 11 and 12 in the second concession to the trustees of the congregation in Richardson's neighbourhood for the establish-

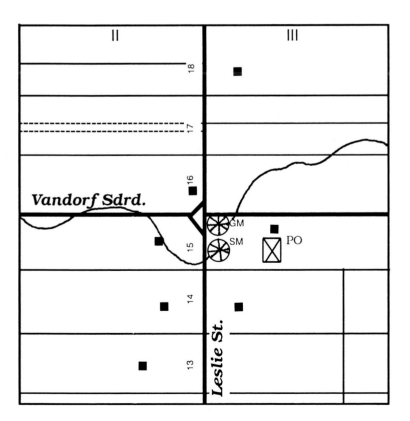

White Rose

Lynne Rubbens

ment of a Methodist church. John Richardson owned property across the road from the new church site.

John Atkinson of Bethesda was the carpenter-contractor for the new church, named Mount Pisgah. It was dedicated for worship at a special service on Wednesday, October 19, 1870, at 10:30 a.m. Following the service, dinner was served in the church basement at a cost of 40 cents a ticket. This was followed by an afternoon session, which featured several addresses given by well-known speakers.

For many years the church was part of a three-point charge (three congregations served by one minister), including both the Temperanceville and the Wesley churches. In 1889 an organ was purchased for the church; prior to this the precentor, or leader of the singing, conducted the hymns. Familiar White Rose family names occur in the early listings of church workers: Jared Lloyd, Stephen Wallace, as well as members of the Smith, Evans, and Forrester families.

Mount Pisgah Church
Whitchurch-Stouffville Museum

IN 1925, with the coming of Church Union, the former Methodist church became the Mount Pisgah United Church and continued to serve its mainly agricultural congregation for many years, providing both religious and social functions. By the 1960s, however, it was apparent that the diminishing congregation could no longer continue to maintain the church. On June 30, 1965, the last regular Sunday service was held; the final One-hundredth Anniversary service was held on October 18, 1970. At this time it was regretfully decided that because of vandalism, the building could no longer be maintained, and both building and furnishings were auctioned off the following May. The church was demolished shortly thereafter.

Early White Rose families sent their children to a schoolhouse built on the northwest corner of lot 9, concession 3, about 1850. This property belonged to Samuel Siddons and his wife, Margaret, who deeded the land to the trustees of School Section #6 (see Appendix B). Apparently Samuel Siddons repurchased this quarter-acre lot sometime before 1863 since an indenture dated February 1863 details an agreement entered into between Samuel Siddons and the trustees of S.S. #6, whereby the trustees agreed to rent the land from S. Siddons at a yearly rent of 50 cents and also to erect a fence around the property to protect the adjoining land. In 1869 S. Siddons turned over his interest in this property to John Smith for the sum of $1.

In 1872 the first schoolhouse was replaced with a new frame building, which was in use until 1945. On January 30, 1945, the building burnt down. The eleven students enrolled at the school continued their education in the basement of the Mount Pisgah United Church and at S.S. #7 (Lloyd School).

In 1948 a frame building was erected on lot 10, concession 2, at the southwest corner of the Bloomington Sideroad and Leslie Street, This school closed on June 29, 1965. At the time of publication this building remains standing, in very poor repair.

S.S. #6, White Rose School, built 1872, burned 1945.
Whitchurch-Stouffville Museum

As a community White Rose has ceased to exist. The mills, post office, church, and school have all disappeared, leaving Leslie Street as a rural road now lying within the borders of the Town of Aurora.

PETCHVILLE

The community of Petchville is located at the corner of the Aurora Sideroad and Leslie Street (the third concession road). The name was derived from the family of Jonathan Petch who, with his wife, Sarah (Gale) Petch, first settled on lot 21, concession 3, in 1818. Jonathan, born in 1778, had been a ship's carpenter with the English navy during the Napoleonic Wars and had immigrated to Canada in 1817 with his wife and children.

Because the lot that Jonathan had chosen to farm was a clergy reserve, he was not able to purchase the property until 1840, when he paid 175 pounds for the 200-acre parcel. Four years later, Jonathan's son, Isaac, had a squared-timber log house built on the north half of his father's property. This house, along with the surrounding property (lot 21 north), was owned and farmed by Isaac and members of his family until it was sold out of the Petch family in 1903. The Crawford family lived here for many years in the first half of the twentieth century. Both William Crawford and his son John held several positions on the Whitchurch Township Council. The log house remained in the Crawford family until 1946. Several families have occupied the old log house in the ensuing years, and as of the date of publication, it remains standing, with renovations and additions, on its original site.

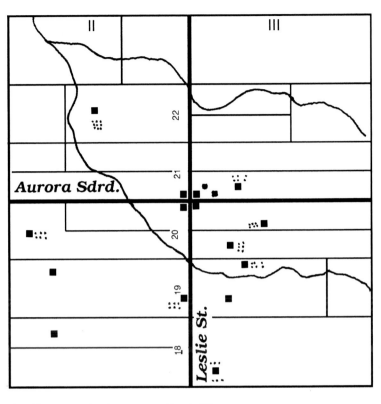

Petchville
Lynne Rubbens

The south half of the original purchase (lot 21 south) remained in the Petch family until 1989. At the time of its sale, it was still being farmed by a Petch, George Robert (Bob), Jonathan's great-great-grandson. Over the years several parcels of land were either sold or deeded away (including the site of Wesley Church). The construction of Highway 404 severed the farm, leaving only 36 acres from Jonathan's original 200. The brick house that fronts on the Aurora Sideroad was built in 1916 and was the Petch family home until 1990.

The south side of the Aurora Sideroad also bore the Petch name for many years. Lot 20, north concession 3, was purchased by Isaac Petch from the Lyon estate, probably about 1874, when his oldest son, Arthur, married. In 1882, when Isaac's youngest son, William, married and took over the family farm on lot 21 north, a brick house was built on lot 20 north, facing the Aurora Sideroad, for Isaac and his wife, Emma (Hacking). They remained there until their deaths in 1899 and 1904 respectively.

Several parcels of land were separated from the original acreage. One parcel, on the southwest corner of lot 21 south, was deeded by Jonathan Petch to Rachel (Petch) and her husband, William Wells, and remained in the Wells family for many years. Their white stucco house remains standing just west of the Petch farmhouse.

A parcel of land on the southeast corner of lot 21 was given for the building of a church in 1847. The Petch family retained strong ties with Wesley Methodist (now United) Church, and when the log church was replaced by a brick building in 1881, the original church was moved to the Petch farm, where it was incorporated into the barn. Many members of the Petch family are interred in the cemetery alongside the church, the earliest burial being that of Jonathan's daughter, Rachel, who died in 1834 at the age of fifteen and was buried on the family farm.

ROBT. LIVINGSTON,
CARRIAGE MAKER,
HORSE SHOER AND GENERAL BLACKSMITH.

☞ Reaping Machines, Thrashing Machines and all Agricultural Implements repaired on Short Notice.

WORKSHOP AT PETCHVILLE, WHITCHURCH.

ABOVE: From Illustrated Historical Atlas of County of York, *1878.*
BELOW: Petch home, built 1916.
Whitchurch-Stouffville Museum

Petchville was apparently also known as Goosetown for part of its history. The *Aurora Banner* of May 2 and June 27, 1890, includes local news columns from the community of Goosetown reporting various happenings there. By July 25, 1890, however, the column that highlighted news of a light potato and apple crop was headed "Petchville."

Lot 20, concession 2 (on the southwest corner of Leslie Street and the Aurora Sideroad), is shown as being part of the estate of the late Joseph Hartman on the 1860 map. However, by 1878 John Usherwood had purchased this property, and he is listed in the 1878 *Illustrated Historical Atlas of the County of York* as a farmer and one of "The Principal Professional Business Men and Farmers of The County Who Patronize This Atlas." The corner of this farm, which includes the southwest corner of the community of Petchville, appears to have been a farmer's field for most of its history.

On the northwest corner of the Petchville crossroads (lot 21, concession 2) was a blacksmith's shop belonging to Robert Livingston. He also is on the Patrons list in the 1878 *Historical Atlas*. Livingston's blacksmith's shop remained at this site until the early 1900s. The lot is at present occupied by a machine shop.

Several newer homes have been added to the hamlet of Petchville, including a large red brick house fronting on the Aurora Sideroad just west of Isaac Petch's 1882 home.

An attractive white frame house, reportedly built in the 1860s, faces Leslie Street at the southeast corner of Petchville. Although little is known of its history, this piece of property appears to have gone through several changes of ownership during the mid-1800s. Thomas Porritt, a blacksmith, and Charles Rahm (or Raham), a carpenter, are two artisans who apparently owned property in this area. An advertisement in the January 2, 1867, edition of the *Aurora Banner* announcing that Henry Harthong of Petchville was in need of a wagon maker identifies another artisan working in the hamlet.

Children from the Petchville area attended S.S. #1 at Hartman's Corners (the intersection of Aurora Sideroad and Bayview Avenue). The first Hartman School was built on lot 81, concession 1, fronting on Bayview Avenue just north of the Aurora Sideroad. The Hartman name came from the Hartman family who owned several farms in the vicinity.

Threshing gang on Peter Graham's farm, lot 23, concession 3.
Whitchurch-Stouffville Museum

The date of this early school is not known: however, according to the *Journals of Upper Canada Legislative Assembly*, a school on lot 81, concession 1 Whitchurch, is among the "Common Schools in Whitchurch Who Have Received the Government Allowance for the Six Months Ending June 30, 1838" and again for the six-month period ending in December 1838. According to their records the teacher for the first six-month period was Martin Young, and there were forty pupils attending. For the second six-month period the teacher was James Hugh and the enrolment thirty-two.

In 1883 a contract was let to Joseph Hall to build a new schoolhouse at a cost of $1,790. It was erected on a new site, lot 21 of the second concession, fronting on the Aurora Sideroad

RIGHT: *Frame house at Petchville.*
BELOW: *S.S. #1, Hartman School, built 1883, demolished 1952.*
Whitchurch-Stouffville Museum

(just east of Bayview Avenue). The old schoolhouse was sold to George W. Graham for $45. He moved the building to Aurora, where it still stands as a residence on Wellington Street East.

The 1883 school was demolished, and a new brick building was erected on the site in 1952. An article in a 1952 edition of the *Aurora Banner* described the new building as built "in a smart modernistic design." The new school provided its forty-two students with up-to-date equipment and furnishings and was designed to serve the community for many years into the future. The formation of the York Region Board of Education resulted in the closure of many rural schools, however, and the last school records available from the Hartman school date from 1965. The building is still owned by the York Region Board of Education and is now used by their Works Department.

In 1971, with the introduction of Regional Government, Petchville ceased to be a part of Whitchurch Township and formed part of the Town of Aurora. Since that time development has moved ever closer to the tiny hamlet, and at the time of publication much of the property has been sold and is awaiting development. A mall proposal has been submitted for the site of Jonathan Petch's original land purchase. Even the white frame house on Leslie Street has been sold, and its future remains in doubt.

BOGARTTOWN

Located around the intersection of today's Leslie Street and Vivian Road/Mulock Drive, Bogarttown was first settled by the Bogart family, hence the name of the hamlet. The Bogarts emigrated from Holland in 1640 and settled near Albany and Brooklyn, New York. Later some family members moved to Pennsylvania.

In the late eighteenth century, Martin Bogart travelled to Upper Canada from Pennsylvania in search of land and mill sites. He returned home, and although he died about 1800, his son, John, migrated to Canada in 1802. John brought his wife, Mary (Opp), his mother, Mary (Cocks), and his six children to the southwest corner of Leslie Street and today's Mulock Drive (lot 30, concession 2).

John's younger brother, Martin, and his family also settled in Whitchurch. The Bogarts immigrated to Upper Canada with Timothy Rogers, the Quaker who was Newmarket's first settler.

In 1803 the northwest corner of Leslie Street and Mulock Drive (lot 31, concession 2) was sold to Hugh Shaw by the Crown. The same year Shaw sold fifty acres of the west side of the lot to Martin Bogart, and the remaining 150 acres to John.

John Bogart built his first sawmill in 1805 and erected a grist mill in 1806. A two-storey frame house was built in 1811, replacing the Bogarts' log home. The frame house was a local curiosity, as there were few others in the area. This Bogart home is still inhabited.

Bogart's son John, Jr., was a township warden for Whitchurch between 1825 and 1830. John, Jr., erected a large frame mill in 1830. The grist mill served the local area, but flour was also exported overseas via Montreal. Area residents also visited the millpond in the winter to cut ice.

With the Bogart mills as the impetus Bogarttown grew, and soon the hamlet boasted a wheelwright shop, a carpenter shop, a tailor shop, a shoemaker, store, as well as a brick blacksmith's shop. Joseph H. Wilkin advertised in 1878 his carriage and wagon shop at lot 32, concession 3. The blacksmith's shop was at lot 31, concession 3. Both shops faced Leslie Street, which was then called Queen Street. The blacksmith's shop can still be found on the

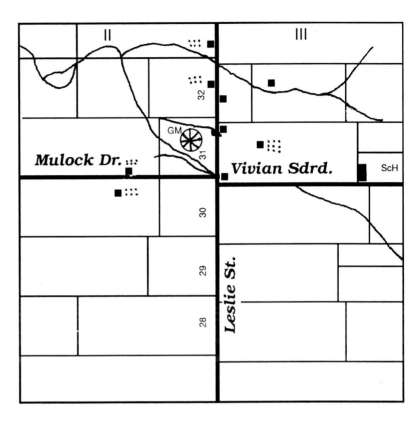

ABOVE: *Bogarttown.* Lynne Rubbens
BELOW: *Interior Bogarttown School, c. 1957.* Whitchurch-Stouffville Museum

Francis Starr's residence, built about 1875 at Bogarttown.
Whitchurch-Stouffville Museum

Bogart Town Mills
NEAR NEWMARKET.
These Mills have lately been purchased by the proprietor.
GRISTING AT THE SHORTEST NOTICE,
AND IN THE BEST MANNER.
FIRST CLASS FLOUR AND FEED, CONSTANTLY ON HAND
AT THE LOWEST CASH PRICE.
J. B. PETHERAM.

JOSEPH H. WILKIN,
Carriage & Waggon Builder,
LUMBER WAGGONS WARRANTED FOR TWO YEARS
GUARANTEED EQUAL TO ANY IN THE COUNTY.'
☞ **HORSE SHOEING A SPECIALTY.**
Workshop at Bogart Town, near MARKHAM.

From Illustrated Historical Atlas of County of York, 1878. Whitchurch-Stouffville Museum

east side of Leslie Street. Queen Street was also the location of two hotels. Bogarttown grew so rapidly that by 1850 its mills and residences rivalled those found in Newmarket.

Bogarttown was doing a larger volume of business than Newmarket, when, in 1853, the Ontario, Simcoe and Huron Railway was built from Toronto, passing through Newmarket. As a result, Bogarttown suffered a setback that it never fully recovered from, allowing Newmarket to develop into a much larger commercial centre. In 1890 Bogarttown obtained a post office, but as rural free delivery became common, it was eventually phased out.

The first school for School Section #3 was located on lot 28 east of the third concession, fronting on Woodbine Avenue. This school apparently served both Bogarttown and Pine Orchard, although both these communities built new schools to serve their respective communities in 1856–57.

The new Bogarttown school was located in the centre of lot 31, concession 3, fronting on the Bogarttown Sideroad (Mulock Drive/Vivian Road). The first teacher at this new red brick building was Francis Starr, who was also a farmer in Bogarttown. The Bogarttown school was also used for Sunday school for many years as the Bogarttown Union Sabbath School. A basement was excavated in 1935 and an addition constructed in 1957.

The school ceased to operate in 1969, and in 1971 the building was sold to the Town of Whitchurch-Stouffville for use as the Whitchurch-Stouffville Museum. The museum operated in this location until 1979, when it was moved to the hamlet of Vandorf in order to make way for the construction of Highway 404. At present the Bogarttown School, reputedly the oldest-standing brick schoolhouse in Southern Ontario, houses the museum's exhibit areas.

The community of Bogarttown became part of the Town of Newmarket with the creation of the Regional Municipality of York in 1971.

GORMLEY

The community of Gormley survives today despite being bypassed, divided by the railway and split in two by Highway 404. Located on the south side of the Stouffville/Gormley Sideroad at Woodbine Avenue (the fourth concession road), Gormley's Corners developed around James Gormley's general store and post office. Gormley had arrived in the area in the 1840s and combined the professions of teacher, auctioneer, and notary public along with those of storekeeper and postmaster.

Earlier settlers, such as the Heises, Brillingers, Steckleys, Cobers, Doners, and Widemans, arrived between 1800 and 1804 and worked hard to clear the land of the black ash that flourished in the area. Fast-flowing streams powered several sawmills, most of which were located on the fourth and fifth concessions. These mills, operated by the Brillingers, Clubines, Bruce brothers, and the Smith family, among others, also provided employment for coopers, shingle makers, wagon makers, carpenters, builders, and a planing mill that produced lath. A cheese factory was opened on the east half of lot 1, concession 4, in the 1860s. Alex Duncan, a local blacksmith, made the cheese presses. William Smith, David Reesor, and Robert and Alex Bruce were some of the various owners during the following thirty-five years. The building was also operated as a woodwork and wagon-making shop for several years.

Gormley
Lynne Rubbens

Agriculture formed the backbone of the community, with a small commercial district growing up around Gormley's store. A second store operated by Sam Moorby opened directly across the road. Account books remaining in the Moorby family show that the store was operating at least between the years 1867 and 1876.

The Francey family ran a large hotel. Other enterprises included a blacksmith's and cabinetmaker's shop, a shoemaker's shop, carriage making, and weaving. In 1904 telephone service arrived in the bustling community. The original James Gormley store and post office continued to serve the community. Sam Doner, one of a number of postmaster-store owners, operated the business for thirty years, beginning in 1923. In 1935 a fire destroyed the original building. The new building, set on the old foundations and erected in a very similar style, continued to serve as both store and post office until 1967. The entire building was then turned over to the post office, and service continued until 1980, when a new post office was built on Woodbine Avenue. The old post office is currently serving the public as an art gallery. By the 1980s Woodbine Avenue had been realigned and the main thoroughfare of Gormley bypassed, isolating the original centre of the community in a pocket.

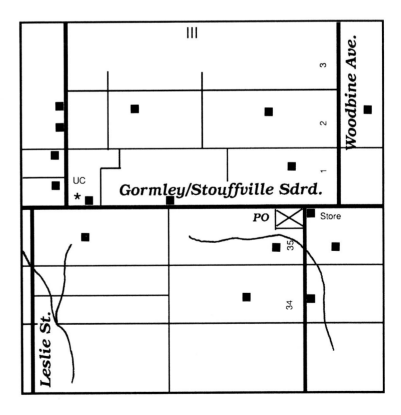

ABOVE: *James Gormley*
BELOW: *Gormley blacksmith's shop*
Whitchurch-Stouffville Museum

The coming of the James Bay Railway in 1905 shifted the business centre of the community to the west by half a concession. A new neighbourhood known as New Gormley grew up around the station. Another store opened in this vicinity, as did a grain elevator, a lumber mill, a harness shop, a blacksmith's shop, a cement block company (operated as the Gormley Block Company for many years) and a short-lived factory that made measuring sticks. A number of substantial homes were also built in this new part of town.

The construction of Highway 404 in 1980 completed the division of Gormley. Passing through the centre of New Gormley, it severed the community, leaving the two sections isolated from each other.

With no school in Gormley itself, children from the community attended one of four rural schools—S.S. #6 (White Rose), or S.S. #7 (Lloyd) in Whitchurch, or one of two Markham schools.

The original S.S. #7 schoolhouse was on the south side of the Bethesda Sideroad at lot 5, concession 3, on property belonging to Thomas Lloyd. It was surrounded by heavy bush and reputed to be very cold and drafty. The earliest records of this school date from 1857.

In December 1902, a decision was made to rebuild the school. A new location was chosen on the north side of the Bethesda Sideroad slightly to the west of the original schoolhouse. Samuel Carlisle and his wife, Ellen, deeded a portion of the west half of lot 6 in the third concession to the trustees of S.S. #7 for the sum of $200. The new school opened in November 1903, having cost a total of $2,843.16. The old building (with furnishings) was sold to Joseph Cherry, who moved it to his farm. The first teacher in the new school was Miss F.E. Richardson. One of the early caretakers was Harry Smith.

In 1946 there were seventeen pupils enrolled, including those attending from S.S. #6 in White Rose, whose new school had not yet been built. That number grew to fifty-five by 1951, so a basement was converted into a second classroom and a new furnace installed. A further two rooms were added to the 1903 building in 1956, and in 1964 the original classroom was refurbished.

When the new area school, Whitchurch Highlands, opened in 1969, S.S. #7 was closed. The building was retained by the Board of Education and is currently used by their Works Department. On November 27, 1969, the old school bell from S.S. #7 was relocated to Whitchurch-Highlands Public School at the official opening.

Religious services for the community were held in a frame church built in 1873 as a community or union church on land donated by John Leary. By the early 1880s pastors from Markham Missionary Church began holding regular services for the Mennonite community in this building. A charter membership was organized in 1891, creating the Gormley United

Gormley general store and post office
Whitchurch-Stouffville Museum

Missionary Church. In 1931 the frame building was replaced by a new brick church, which was completely renovated with the addition of a Christian Education wing in 1966.

Several families from the Gormley area founded an early Brethren in Christ congregation. Although related to the Mennonites, this group differed in several practices, including that of adult baptism by total immersion, which gave them the name Dunkards. A similar closely

CLOCKWISE, STARTING FROM TOP LEFT:
**Gormley United Missionary Church, built
1873.**
Demolishing the church in 1931.
"New Gormley."
**"New Gormley" and Gormley train
station.**
Whitchurch-Stouffville Museum

GORMLEY, ONT.

related group also became known as the Tunkers. The Markham Township congregation met
in members' homes from its formation in 1808 until 1877, when a church building was erected
on lot 32, concession 3 Markham, at Heise Hill on Woodbine Avenue south of the Stouffville
Sideroad. A faithful congregation still meets regularly in the original building.

S.S. #7, Lloyd School, built c. 1850.
Whitchurch-Stouffville Museum

Originally situated in Markham Township, the early community of Gormley's Corners became part of Whitchurch-Stouffville in 1971 with the creation of the Region of York. This new system saw the Whitchurch-Markham boundary moved south of the original town line (Stouffville/Gormley Sideroad) to avoid dividing communities. However, since Highway 404 provides the boundary line between Whitchurch-Stouffville and Richmond Hill, Gormley finds itself once again divided between two neighbouring towns.

PRESTON LAKE

All three of the names Lake Reesor, Middleton Lake, and Preston Lake refer to the body of water and community located at the northeast corner of Woodbine Avenue (the fourth concession road) and the Bloomington Sideroad.

Known now as Preston Lake, the lake was originally called Reesor Lake after the family that owned 200 acres north of the lake and 200 acres south on the Bloomington Sideroad.

Frederic Baron de Hoen was granted 2600 acres in Whitchurch Township, mostly in the area of the lake, in 1802. In particular, he owned lots 10 and 11, concession 4. He received the grants as a Hessian soldier who had served with the British army in the American War of Independence. Through the years a story has been handed down that he sold those 400 acres of land for the cost of a horse and saddle to Peter Reesor, a Pennsylvania German, who registered the land in 1805. Reesor and his family and many others moved from Pennsylvania to settle in the area in 1803. The area, thick with dense bush, was settled by other Mennonite families, such as the Tauns and Brillingers, between 1850 and 1900.

The lake was known at the beginning of the century as Middleton Lake after the family of the same name. The Middletons sold their land to George Preston, making him the major landowner around the lake. He purchased the 200 acres just after 1900 and developed the lake as a summer tourist resort in the early 1920s. In 1915 Preston built a huge red brick, eleven-room farmhouse to the north of lot 13, which still stands in 1993. The residence became the first to have electricity in the area in 1923, operating on a generator (a Delco system) set up in the basement. Preston even used his home as a hotel in the summers of the 1920s. When the tourists arrived, his family would live in the basement. The lane to his house was the only access road to the lake during the 1920s, and Preston picked up a toll of 25 cents for cars and 10 cents for horses and carriages on their way to the lake. In 1931 Preston began developing the north side of the lake, hiring engineers and surveyors to draw up plans for lots. Preston created two beaches, one private and one public, and installed a wharf and diving facility for swimmers. He stocked the lake with bass for fishing. Preston did not limit himself to development: he was also a thrasher, a steam-engine salesman, a farmer, and at one time a school-board member.

The lake also had a number of dance halls built in the early part of the century—which eventually burnt down, the last in the late 1950s.

After the Second World War, Preston moved his main cottage to the west side of the lake, dragging it across the lake in the winter by sleigh. Halfway across, workers left the building for the night; the next morning they were forced to extract it from melting ice.

The lake area was immortalized by the Group of Seven artist A.J.

Preston Lake
Lynne Rubbens

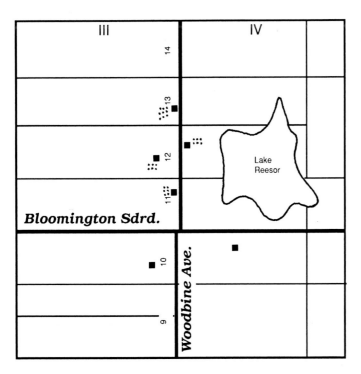

Casson, who painted the Hennessy homestead in 1955. The house no longer resembles that in the Casson painting, but still stands in 1993 on the west side of Woodbine Avenue directly opposite a lakefront subdivision.

Necessities were looked after in the neighbouring hamlet of Vandorf, which had the general store and post office, school and church. During the 1920s and 1930s the area was inhabited mainly by farmers, and tourists and cottagers during the summer. By the 1950s people began to live year-round at the fifty-acre kettle lake. Estate residential homes began cropping up around the lake in the late 1980s, one development replacing a trailer park.

LEFT: ***George and Annie Preston, Preston Lake, summer 1940.*** Rick Preston
ABOVE: ***Preston Lake, c. 1925.*** Landford Preston Lake Project

VANDORF

The Vandorf area was surveyed and parcelled out about 1800 by grant and patent to government favourites, military officers, and Quaker settlers. North of the Vandorf Sideroad, lots 16 to 24, concession 3, totalling 1600 acres, was granted to Capt. William Graham for military service. On the east side lots 18 to 24, concession 4, were granted to Samuel Lundy for his group of Quaker settlers. Deducted from each grant was a 200-acre lot held in reserve for the clergy.

The basic need of the early settlers was water, and here they found a good stream, the east branch of the Holland River, which still flows through the village. At the time of settlement it was much deeper and wider than it is today.

Union Street (as Woodbine Avenue was then known) was little better than a trail. The Quaker settlers used it as a link to a better-known trail that ran from Newmarket to Uxbridge. Many of their friends from Pennsylvania lived along that trail. Another trail led west from Hacking's Corners (now Wesley Corners) to Machell's Corners (now Aurora). Early settlement took place near the stream, to the north of the hill that was the highest point of land on the Oak Ridges moraine and became a natural southern border for the small community originally known as Brookvale.

Settlement continued both on the Graham estate and along the Vandorf Sideroad west to the Lloyd mills at White Rose. To the north of the stream William Williamson purchased lot 18, concession 4, on January 1, 1831. Most of the acreage was in virgin pine; in winter logs were cut and hauled to the nearest mill and sawn into lumber. Several lumber companies until recently occupied that land, on Slater Road. Matthew Williamson purchased lots 17 and 18, concession 3, from the Graham estates, and the farm remained in the Williamson family for many years. It has recently been developed with estate homes.

In 1849 George Snider, Jr., built a woodworking shop on 25 acres of the northwest quarter of lot 16, concession 4, purchased from his father. He had apprenticed as a wheelwright at a shop at Machell's Corners. With his wife, Eliza, he lived in the east end of the shop for six years before building a home to the south of it in 1857. This house still stands and is now a cabinetmaker's shop, thus continuing the woodworking tradition in the village. Over the years George and his son Alfred supplied most of the wooden articles needed by early farmers. They specialized in the manufacture of grain cradles, which were sold over a large area. Wagons and sleighs were made and repaired, as were oxen yokes and bows, well curbs, churns, plain furniture, and axe and fork handles. The company also replaced bottoms in washtubs and pails and sometimes even made coffins. The woodworking shop

Vandorf
Lynne Rubbens

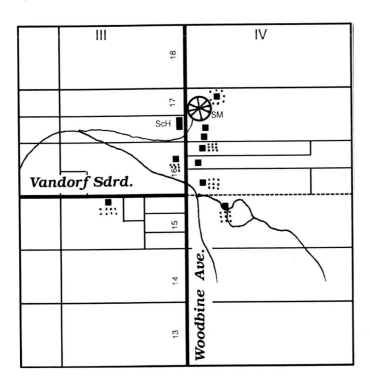

ABOVE LEFT: **Vandorf post office and public library, 1905.** Whitchurch-Stouffville Museum. *ABOVE RIGHT*: **The White House, lot 17, concession 4, Vandorf.** Reta Alcorn. *BELOW*: **Vandorf post office with the Van Nostrand mill to the right.** Whitchurch-Stouffville Museum

ABOVE: Union Street, c. 1910.
BELOW: Vandorf blacksmith's shop and
chopping mill. Mechanic's hall far right.
Whitchurch-Stouffville Museum

was closed in 1907, although the building continued to serve many purposes until it was destroyed by fire in 1982.

When Alfred Snider closed his woodworking shop, he purchased the general store and post office directly across the road. It had been established in 1882 by George Henry Powell, whose father, George Powell, had emigrated from Yorkshire and was granted the southern half of lot 16, concession 4, in 1845. The rear 50 acres were subsequently sold to Thomas Lewis for his sawmill.

George Henry Powell began his business from his father's house, travelling to Toronto twice a week with farm produce to be sold or traded for such goods as cottons, yarn, and thread, which in turn he sold to his neighbours. The Vandorf General Store and the adjoining house were eventually built on the northeast corner of lot 16, concession 3, property that George Powell, Sr., had purchased from the Graham estate in 1868.

When a post office was opened in 1887 in the village store, George Powell was appointed the first postmaster. The request for a post office revealed that the name Brookvale, the one originally chosen for the community, was already in use. A new name had to be selected, so Vandorf was the choice. "Van" was for the Van Nostrand family, owners of the sawmill, and "dorf" means village in Dutch.

A sawmill had existed in Vandorf since the 1840s, when Dr. James Hunter of Newmarket established two mills along the fast-flowing stream, one in the fifth concession and the other on Woodbine Avenue in the centre of the present community. In 1855 the mill site and with lot 15, concession 4, were sold to John Van Nostrand and George Harrison, brothers-in-law and former mill owners in York Mills just north of Toronto. They brought their families to Vandorf early in 1856. The Harrisons moved into a small frame house, which still forms the centre part of the residence known locally as the White House, on lot 17. The Van Nostrands moved into a slightly smaller frame-and-plank farmhouse on lot 15. Descendants of John Van Nostrand continue to occupy both home and farm. Eventually John Van Nostrand bought out the Harrisons' share of the business and moved his family into the White House, which was enlarged to accommodate his nine children and mill workers. The home remained in the

Van Nostrand family for many years after John's death in 1895. In the 1930s it operated as a men's hostel. At the present time the White House remains standing in the village core.

Soon after John Van Nostrand's death, the mill was closed, the mill yard was gradually cleared of old lumber piles, and the mill was demolished. It provided a building site for the present-day community hall after the old Mechanics Hall was burnt in 1921. Other buildings occupying the former mill site are two homes and the former municipal offices for the Township of Whitchurch.

A blacksmith's shop operated in the mill yard until 1870, when, as the result of a fire, it was relocated to lot 16, concession 4, in the centre of the village. William Pettit was the blacksmith. After the mill closed, Pettit purchased the lot with the blacksmith's shop. He demolished the old shop and built his own which he operated until 1903. It continued to be a blacksmith's shop for nearly forty years under various blacksmiths. It was a substantial stone building with a large room above, which was used as a lodge room and meeting place by the Knights of the Maccabees (a secret charitable society) and other groups. The building was demolished in 1952.

In 1905 the James Bay Railway purchased land from many village farms for the right of way. Construction continued for several years, and a station was built at Vandorf. This line was later taken over by the Canadian National Railways and remains a part of their network. The station had an agent-telegrapher for many years. This service was discontinued and the station demolished in 1967.

Children from the Vandorf area attended S.S. #2 in the village. Although there are reports of an early common school (welcoming all neighbourhood children) as far back as 1833, its exact location is unknown. By 1878 the Vandorf school was located on lot 17, east concession 3, fronting on the present Woodbine Avenue directly across from the Van Nostrand sawmill. The first school apparently was built slightly north of the existing building. It was a small frame building and was used until the present structure was erected in 1870. Property was bought from George Powell and from John Williamson for the schoolhouse. The original building was frame, with two entrances and heated by a wood-burning box stove. In 1905 the school was remodelled. It was raised, with a basement added, and bricked on the outside. The two front entrances were closed and a central door made, with an outside stair. A furnace was installed in the basement along with cloak rooms and a play area. In 1936 the school was wired for electricity, indoor toilets were installed in 1942, and an oil furnace replaced the coal furnace in 1950.

In 1956 a decision was made to build a new school on a site on the east side of Woodbine Avenue, slightly south of the 1870 building. Unlike the first structure, this one did not front on Woodbine Avenue but stood back slightly from the road. Overcrowding became a problem for the two-room school in the 1960s, so in 1965 two portable classrooms were added. The school was closed in June 1970 when the York Region Board of Education was established. It was sold in 1972 and has been used for various purposes since then.

ABOVE: **Vandorf train station, c. 1911.**
Whitchurch-Stouffville Museum
BELOW: **Vandorf community hall.** Staley
family collection
ABOVE RIGHT: **Vandorf Public School, S.S.
#2, c. 1890.** Whitchurch-Stouffville
Museum

The 1870 schoolhouse on the west side of Woodbine Avenue had several tenants after 1956, one being the Ontario Provincial Police. In 1979 the school became the property of the Town of Whitchurch-Stouffville and became part of the Whitchurch-Stouffville Museum, as did the Bogarttown school, which was moved to the site. The museum currently uses the Vandorf school building as an activity room and storage facility.

The Vandorf community park south of the museum was once part of the Powell farm. A low field, it was not arable but was an excellent cow pasture. George Powell planted the old willow trees along the stream to shade and protect it in times of drought. The property was 11 acres and was later purchased for use as a cow pasture by Michael Guthrie, who farmed the southern half of lot 20, concession 4. After Guthrie's death the township council purchased it and established a park board. Over the years the park has evolved into a popular setting for picnics and recreation.

Telephones arrived in Vandorf in 1905, hydroelectricity in 1929. With the advent of the automobile several gas stations opened in town, at first in front of the general store, then in 1924 in a new location south of the Vandorf Sideroad on the west side of Woodbine Avenue. Road widening in 1952 forced the business to be relocated across the road to a new building owned by members of the Van Nostrand family until 1988.

The lumbering business returned to Vandorf after the Second World War. In 1947 the Slater's mill was set up beyond the railway station on Slater's Road east of Woodbine Avenue and several lumber industries were until recently on the property where William Williamson cut and hauled logs more than 150 years ago.

Today Vandorf is experiencing new growth. Family farms are fast disappearing and new residents are moving into homes being built on former fields and meadows. A number of companies have located in the business park on the east side of Woodbine Avenue. Traffic flows through the village past the heritage homes and buildings that remain to remind us of the past.

WESLEY CORNERS

The name Wesley Corners was derived from Wesley Church, situated at the crossroads of the Aurora Sideroad and Woodbine Avenue (the fourth concession road). Before the first church was built about 1840, this crossroads was known as Hacking's Corners.

Rev. James Hacking brought his family from Yorkshire, England, and settled on lots 21 and 22, concession 4, about 1817. He was a Congregational local preacher and held meetings in his own home. The saddlebag preachers of the Yonge Street circuit knew it as Hacking's Meeting House.

James Hacking, with some members of his family, moved to Peel County, where he continued to preach, but his son, John, remained to clear the farms and start a family. A small store was operated by the Hackings to supply the basic needs of the growing community, thereby saving area residents a trip to Machell's Corners (Aurora).

Jonathan Petch of lot 21, concession 3, donated a half-acre lot from the rear southeast corner of his farm for a log church, appropriately known as Petch's Chapel. It served the community for forty years before being replaced by the new Methodist church, built in 1881. From this time the name of the community gradually changed to Wesley, the name given to the church to honour Rev. John Wesley, founder of the Methodist movement.

Wesley United Church is situated a mile north of the village of Vandorf where the Aurora Sideroad intersects Woodbine Avenue. People have gathered there for worship and fellowship since the early days of settlement. The first church stood on the site of the present building and was of hewn-log construction, covered with half-inch siding on the outside and measuring 40 feet long by 30 feet wide. It had one centre aisle with a high pulpit at the north end, reached by several steps. The choir occupied the northwest corner and sat facing the minister. John Petch, the choir leader, acted as precentor and, with the aid of a tuning fork, led the congregation in the singing of hymns.

Wesley Corners
Lynne Rubbens

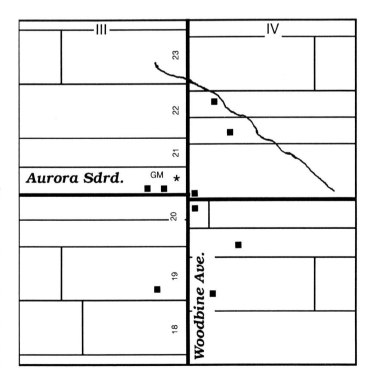

The first organ was purchased about 1870, although some members opposed the very presence of a musical instrument in the house of God. The men sat on one side of the church, the ladies on the other, on hand-made benches that remained in use until 1956.

At a meeting on January 4, 1881, church trustees agreed to erect a new church. The six members of the building committee accomplished the tremendous task of construction in eleven months. On Thursday, December 22, 1881, the new Wesley Methodist Church was dedicated to the worship of God at an eleven o'clock service. A dinner (tickets cost 25 cents), bazaar, and platform meeting followed, at which an appeal for subscriptions to eliminate the remaining debt was so successful that the entire amount was provided, with a substantial profit on the side. The total cost of the new church, including furnishings, was $2,700. The first sabbath meetings were held on Sunday, December 25, at 10:30 a.m., 2:30 and 6:30 p.m.

In 1887 Wesley Church became part of the Temperanceville Circuit, sharing the services of one minister with the Mount Pisgah and Temperanceville churches, and in 1925, with Church Union, became Wesley United Church.

In the years since the early residents of Hackings Corners first worshipped in their homes, the church at Wesley Corners has been a centre for community functions and social fellowship as well as worship. It remains standing in 1993, much as it appeared at its dedication service in 1881, still maintained by a small congregation.

In 1955 the east area of lot 20, concession 3, was surveyed into residential lots. There were twenty-three lots in the subdivision, named Wesley Park, south of the Aurora Sideroad on the west side of Woodbine Avenue. The first home was built in 1957. A service station at the intersection and a park area were incorporated into the plan. Five residential lots were also

ABOVE: Mary Hacking, wife of John Hacking, Jr. BELOW: John Hacking, Jr. Whitchurch-Stouffville Museum
ABOVE RIGHT: Wesley Church, 1900. Whitchurch-Stouffville Museum
BELOW RIGHT: Van Nostrand family collection

sold individually from the south half of lot 20, concession 3. Houses built on these lots stretch along the west side of Woodbine Avenue south of the intersection.

Several commercial enterprises have been built around the Wesley Corner intersection. At the time of publication, much of the remaining farmland has been sold and is awaiting development.

PLEASANTVILLE

A crossroads hamlet, Pleasantville grew around the corner of Woodbine Avenue and Bogarttown Sideroad (Vivian Road).

The original landowners were Quakers, especially on the east side of the hamlet. Some families who settled the area included the Widdifields, Tooles, Willsons, Lundys, and Starrs. Pleasant Valley was reputedly the original name of the settlement.

The property on the northwest corner of the intersection (lot 31, concession 3 east), was known as Pleasant House or Pleasantville Corner. William Widdifield operated a blacksmith's shop on the property in the 1890s. Pleasantville's post office was opened in Pleasant House in 1908. The post office operated for only six years and was closed when rural mail delivery was instituted in 1914. Dan Lundy was the first of only two postmasters, followed by Nelson Collingwood.

The children of Pleasantville did not have a school of their own to attend; rather, they went to school with those from Bogarttown (S.S. #3).

Col. William H. Beresford purchased the southwest corner of Woodbine Avenue and Vivian Road (lot 30, concession 3 east). In

LEFT: Colonel Beresford's mud house, 1838, lot 30, concession 3, Whitchurch.
Helen Johnston
RIGHT: Pleasantville
Lynne Rubbens

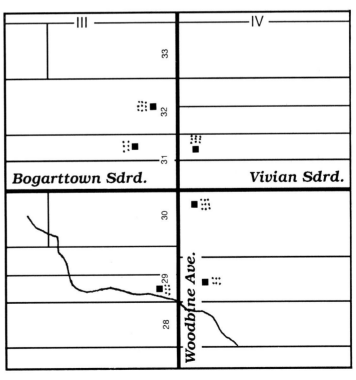

ABOVE: *Home of Elmer and Elma M. Starr, summer of 1915, Newmarket.* Helen Johnston

ABOVE RIGHT: *Pleasantville blacksmith's shop at Union Street (Woodbine Avenue) and Bogarttown Sideroad (William Widdifield).* Whitchurch-Stouffville Museum

BELOW: *Joshua Willson's home, lot 27, concession 4, Whitchurch, 1903.* Helen Johnston

1853 Beresford, an English army officer, built a grand home by the banks of the stream that passed through the property. The walls of the house were made of mud and pea straw, and were 3 feet thick. The building measured approximately 80 feet by 40 feet, with two sections, seven fireplaces, and eighteen rooms, including a ballroom. Beresford's expensive folly eventually impoverished him, the home fell into ruin, and it no longer stands.

Woodbine Avenue became a highway in 1940 and was paved in 1948, helping to usher in change for the tiny hamlet. A fireworks-display company bought property on Vivian Road in 1952, but the business was not successful, and buildings constructed for the company were sold. Not a great deal of the original Pleasantville remains today.

BETHESDA

The community of Bethesda is situated at the four corners of Warden Avenue (the fifth concession road) and the Bethesda Sideroad. The hamlet flourished about 1875, with settlement clustered around the general store and post office, the school and the church. William Hunt's blacksmith's shop and carriage-making shop were both in operation on the southeast corner of the crossroads before 1900.

A Primitive Methodist Church was built in Bethesda in 1855 by John Atkinson, a carpenter who had recently moved to the area. Located on the northwest corner of the crossroads on lot 6, concession 4, the church became the centre for religious activities in the surrounding areas. The Sunday school was formed in 1858 with Mr. Atkinson as superintendent. In 1880 the local Mennonite Church combined with the Methodists to form a Union Sunday School. Isaac Pike served as superintendent of this combined sabbath school for almost fifty years. In 1871 the church was remodelled and improved, and some years later the frame building was bricked. It was in service until 1969, when it was closed. The building remains today, maintained as a private residence.

Not all religious services were held in the church, however. Bethesda became known as a centre for outdoor camp meetings held over a period of several days. Hundreds came from miles around by foot, on horseback, and by carriage and wagon to hear the preaching and to participate in prayer meetings led by Mennonite and Methodist preachers. From the early 1900s to the 1960s, camp meetings were held at Pike's Peak, a hill on Isaac Pike's farm at lot 8, concession 5.

The first store in Bethesda was on the southwest corner of the intersection. Later a new store was built on the north side of the sideroad beside the church. The post office was located in this new store from its opening in 1874, when Hezekiah Pretty was postmaster, until 1924 when the Bethesda post office was closed.

Several buildings housed the Bethesda school (S.S. #12). The original schoolhouse was apparently a log building located on lot 6 west, concession 5. In 1872 a brick schoolhouse was erected farther north on lot 7 west, concession 5, fronting on Warden Avenue, just north of the Bethesda Sideroad. In this school young Isaac Pike launched his teaching career in 1874. He remained as teacher for the next forty-three years, educating several generations from the same families. A large box stove heated the room, and double desks were shared by older and younger students.

In 1892 the building burnt down. During the rebuilding period children were taught in a shed on Pike's farm. The rebuilt school continued to educate local children until it closed on June 29, 1965. The building served as the Bethesda Emmanuel Church until 1992.

The community of Bethesda gained distinction on March 15, 1904, when the first general meeting of the Bethesda and Stouffville Telephone Association was held. The postmaster W. D. Heise, who operated the general store at Bethesda, provided the impetus for the formation of the private telephone company when he made inquiries concerning the terms under which

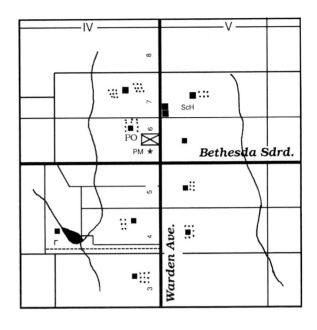

ABOVE: Bethesda. Lynne Rubbens
BELOW: Church and store on left. Hunt's blacksmith's shop on right. Whitchurch-Stouffville Museum

BETHESDA, ONT

73

Methodist Church — Bethesda, Ont.

ABOVE: ***Bethesda Methodist church before remodelling.*** Markham District Historical Museum

RIGHT: ***Bethesda School. Isaac Pike taught all these students.***

BELOW: ***Bethesda and Stouffville telephone company directory.*** Whitchurch-Stouffville Museum

The Bethesda and Stouffville Telephone Company, Limited

Stouff. 3614	Bruce, A. D. ......Pres. & Mgr.	Unionville, R.R.
" 1801	Sangster, Dr. W. A. .....Vice-Pres.	Stouffville
" 6303	Heise, David W. ......Secretary	Gormley, R.R. 1
" 101	Ratcliff, Jas. H. ......Treasurer	Stouffville
" 162	Jennings, Thos. ......Superintendent	Stouffville
" 151	Rae, Thos. B. ......Accountant	Stouffville
" 17502	Garage & Storeroom	Stouffville

EXCHANGES AT
STOUFFVILLE, CLAREMONT, RICHMOND HILL
AND AURORA

Agents for the BELL TELEPHONE CO. IN STOUFFVILLE AND CLAREMONT.

CONTINUOUS SERVICE.

CHRISTMAS DAY SERVICE 10c. per call.

NIGHT SERVICE, 9.30 p.m. to 6.30 a.m., when the charge is 10c. for each exchange through which the call passes.

SUNDAY SERVICE, calls during the day service 5c. per call.

BELL TELEPHONE CONNECTIONS: Long Distance Bell Connection can be obtained via Stouffville, Richmond Hill and Aurora Exchanges.

CLAREMONT SUBSCRIBERS may be listed either in the Bethesda and Stouffville Telephone Company Section or in the Home Telephone Company Section.

LIST OF PLACES
Which the Independent Lines Reach

———

BETHESDA AND STOUFFVILLE LINE

Almira	Buttonville	Gormley	Richmond Hill
Altona	Church Hill	Goodwood	Stouffville
Atha	Claremont	Headford	Thornhill
Aurora	Cashel	Lemonville	Unionville
Bethesda	Dollar	Mongolia	Vandorf
Ballantrae	Elgin Mills	Oak Ridges	Victoria Square
Bloomington	Glasgow	Ringwood	White Rose

the Bell Telephone Company would serve Bethesda. Since Bell's terms were not acceptable, a movement was started to form a private organization composed of subscribers who would install their own telephone system. Originally it was expected that this local system would connect to the Bell Telephone Company for exchange service and for long-distance service. When this proved impossible, the B. & S. Telephone Association established its own exchange in Ratcliff & Co.'s grocery store in the village of Stouffville. On August 1, 1904, the first telephone was installed in David Heise's house at Bethesda. By 1905 the system had been extended to Markham village with forty-one telephones in service and orders for six more. By 1906, when the lines were extended to Gormley, there were 110 subscribers. A night operator was engaged in 1911. Prior to this the night line had been operated from James Ratcliff's bedroom, often robbing him of sleep.

The local company continued to expand its services into Richmond Hill and Vandorf and initiated the formation of an independent telephone union, comprising eleven private systems. By 1930 the total number of telephones using the B. & S. system was 1188, the highest number in the history of the company. A.D. Bruce was president of the company during its first fifty years of operation. In May 1960, the Bell Telephone Company purchased the entire system of the Bethesda and Stouffville Telephone Company, and the local company ceased operation.

Although installation of a telephone service brought the world closer to Bethesda's doorstep, daily life continued to follow the regular routine. Winter months meant skating and hockey on Pike's Pond and tobogganing at Atkinson's hill. Summer saw church garden parties and strawberry festivals, and year-round neighbours helped neighbours. Today the church, store, and school buildings remain, all privately owned, and a golf course has replaced the blacksmith's shop and store on the southwest corner.

PINE ORCHARD

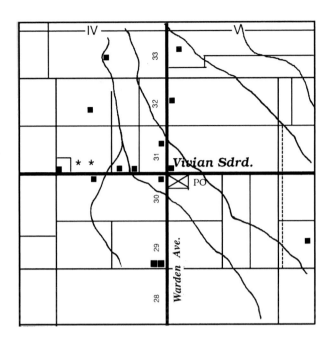

The hamlet of Pine Orchard was originally a Quaker settlement lying approximately 4 miles east of Newmarket at the intersection of Warden Avenue (the fifth concession road) and the Vivian Sideroad.

Although Quakers in Pennsylvania and New Jersey did not suffer persecution during or after the American Revolution on account of their non-combatant status, lawlessness and oppressive taxation persuaded many of them to head north across the border in search of a new life in Upper Canada. They were shrewd, industrious, sober-minded, and familiar with conditions in the backwoods. Samuel Lundy was one such person.

In 1802 he and Isaac Phillips, from Muncy County, Pennsylvania, applied to Lt.-Gov. Peter Hunter for a grant of twenty parcels of land of 200 acres each on the third, fourth, and fifth concessions of Whitchurch, promising at the time to secure the necessary settlers to clear the land. A clause in the grant stated that 10 acres were to be cleared (to farm) and fenced; a log or frame structure of 16 by 20 feet with a shingle roof had to be constructed; all timber in front of and the whole width of the lot had to be cleared, with 35 feet to be cleared and left for half the public road. This formidable task was to be accomplished within two years.

In the winter of 1802 a small band of settlers arrived from Pennsylvania to take possession of their new homesteads. Some of the original families in the area were the Lundys, Tooles, Widdifields, Boughstanchs, Clines, Playters, Lloyds, Randalls, and Willsons.

They worshipped at first in their homes, and subsequently plans were laid for a meeting house. In 1814 Samuel Lundy sold part of his farm to the community for use as a building site and burying ground (part of lot 31, concession 4). By 1827 it was felt that a larger building was needed, and it was constructed east of the original meeting house. During the Hicksite Separation of the Friends, a schism between orthodox Quakers and a progressive group called the Hicksites in 1828, it was decided that orthodox members would continue to worship in the original meeting house and the Hicksites would occupy the new one.

In 1915 the burying ground was levelled, early stone markers were removed, and the present iron fence was erected. Unfortunately the early burial records are gone, but Samuel Lundy was laid to rest there in 1826. In 1975 a historical marker was erected on the

ABOVE: Pine Orchard. Lynne Rubbens
BELOW: Hicksite Quaker site meeting house. Reverend McMath starting renovations in 1944. Original built in 1829-30. Helen Johnston

*ABOVE: **Mule and scraper digging out for the basement, October 1944.***
*BELOW: **Edwin Lundy home before repairs.***
Helen Johnston

Pine Orchard Union Church grounds commemorating the Whitchurch Quaker Settlement, and two years later services were discontinued. The small meeting house was moved to Aurora. The building still stands on the west side of Yonge Street north of Reuben Street, but is now a commercial property.

By mid-century Pine Orchard was beginning to emerge as a small but viable community. With the establishment of the first post office, it became an official settlement in 1853. The *Canadian Directory of 1858* lists Pine Orchard as a village approximately 30 miles north of Toronto with a population of thirty-five. By 1920 the population had only increased to forty.

Moses Willson, the first postmaster, ran a general store on the northwest corner of the Vivian Sideroad and Kennedy Road (the sixth concession road). In 1862 Willson sold the store and one acre of land to Joseph Taylor. Mail was being delivered from Newmarket tri-weekly by this time. In 1874 the post office was again moved, to the southeast corner of Warden Avenue (the fifth concession road) and the Vivian Sideroad, on the property of Nelson May (lot 30, concession 5), a carpenter by trade. It was closed in 1914, at his death, and postal service was moved to Cedar Valley approximately one mile east.

By 1860 at least three sawmills were operating in the area: the James Starr property (lot 30, concession 4 east); Edward Randall (lot 30, concession 5 west); and Joseph Taylor (lot 30, concession 6 west). Taylor Creek was dammed about 1860 by Aaron Haines, and a water-driven sawmill at that location was operated by Abraham Taylor. This property was sold many times during the next thirty years, but the grist mill and sawmill continued to operate. By 1902 George Hopper had purchased the property. He rebuilt the grist mill and in 1905 sold a 3-acre parcel to the James Bay Railway. By this time Jesse Lundy had acquired the business and continued to operate the mill until the 1950s.

Harvey Reginald McMillan (of McMillan Bloedel) was born in 1885 on the Samuel Lundy property (lot 32, concession 4 east), the son of Alfred and Joan Wilson McMillan. He attended school at Bogarttown and Sharon and graduated from high school in Aurora. McMillan received a degree from the Ontario Agriculture College in Guelph in 1906. He became one of the richest and most powerful businessman in Canadian history and probably did more to sell British Columbia timber products throughout the world than anyone else, past or present.

In 1850 a piece of land was severed from the property of Watson Playter (lot 29, concession 4) south of the Pine Orchard crossroads, for the first school in the community. The log schoolhouse was built soon afterwards. This first schoolhouse was later replaced by a larger brick building, and, when it became overcrowded, a new red brick school was opened in September 1924, serving children from Grades 1 through 10. This school gathered students from both Pine Orchard and Cedar Valley. With the arrival of regional government, the school was closed and the building sold. It is now maintained as a private residence. The James Bay Railway, running through Cedar Valley, served both communities, and schoolchildren of the period remember riding the morning train to Vandorf, a few miles down the track, for fall fairs at the Vandorf school.

A new tannery and blacksmith's shop were established in 1868 on the William Bassett property (lot 30, concession 5 east), and by 1880 Pine Orchard was a thriving community with grist- and sawmills, a cheese factory, blacksmith's shops, a shoemaker (Reid), a wheel-wright, a fledgling honey and maple syrup industry, and a library. By the turn of the century even the millpond near Cedar Valley was being rented by the Newmarket Fishing Club for $50 annually!

The local Temperance Hall, no longer on the site, north of the Vivian Sideroad on the fifth concession road, was used for political meetings, the local Farmers' Club and church services. Obediah Widdifield was the first chaplain.

The establishment of the Church of Christ at Pine Orchard occurred about 1904, when a few members who lived in the district and were meeting with the Church of Christ in Stouffville felt the need for a local site. Early meetings were held in the home of Brother Charles Brandon, Sr. When the house could no longer accommodate the congregation the Temperance Hall was used as a meeting place. The congregation worshipped at this location for almost nine years prior to the erection of the church building in 1916 on its present site on the west side of Warden Avenue (the fifth concession road) south of the Vivian Sideroad. In 1959–60 a basement was added to enhance facilities.

Pine Orchard School, S.S. #4.
Whitchurch-Stouffville Museum

In 1936 a small service station was built at the southwest corner of the Vivian Sideroad and Warden Avenue (the fifth concession road) and later enlarged to a two-bay garage. The station and an auto refinisher are on the site at publication date. There is also a small variety store and commercial outlet just to the west of the service station. The area is still very sparsely settled.

Paving the Vivian Sideroad in the 1970s did nothing to improve the commercial viability of the small community, and most of the buildings of the bustling 1880s have disappeared.

CEDAR VALLEY

Cedar Valley, situated at the intersection of the Vivian Sideroad and Kennedy Road (the sixth concession road) is only 1 1/4 miles east of Pine Orchard, so it shared local services with that community, which had been building since the mid-1800s.

The post office was moved from Pine Orchard to Cedar Valley in 1908, with Henry Widdifield serving as first postmaster.

The James Bay Railway established a line running north through the western side of Whitchurch in 1905. The line passed to the east side of Cedar Valley, on a right-of-way over the millpond (lot 30, concession 6); however, the station stop was named Pine Orchard. A small grain elevator and loading ramps were available for stock and produce. Although local dairy farmers could readily ship their products to Toronto, commerce in the tiny community did not increase, nor did the population, which hovered for many decades at a number between thirty and forty people. In the 1930s a fire damaged the railway station, and as the CNR added heavier freight to the line, Pine Orchard ceased to be a recognized stop. The station was demolished in the early 1940s.

In 1907 the chopping mill and sawmill on Taylor Creek, which had been in operation for more than fifty years, was bought by Jesse Lundy, who operated it until his death in 1952. During the years from 1910 onward, many local businesses have come and gone, including cement-block manufacturing, egg and honey production, a fertilizer plant, a sod farm, and a potato producer.

Cedar Valley is also the home of the Free Methodist Camp, situated on the north side of the Vivian sideroad just east of Kennedy Road. The camp includes 10 acres of land with cottages, a cookhouse, a large dining room with seating for approximately two hundred and a permanent tabernacle, built in 1952, which seats one thousand people.

Even though the Vivian Sideroad was paved in the late 1970s, the population of Cedar Valley stayed at about 150. Although specific population figures are not available for the 1990s, virtually nothing remains of this small hamlet.

C.N.R. STATION PINE ORCHARD, ONT.

ABOVE: *Cedar Valley.* Lynne Rubbens
BELOW: *Pine Orchard station. James Bay/Canadian Northern Railway, located east of Cedar Valley.* Whitchurch-Stouffville Museum

LEMONVILLE

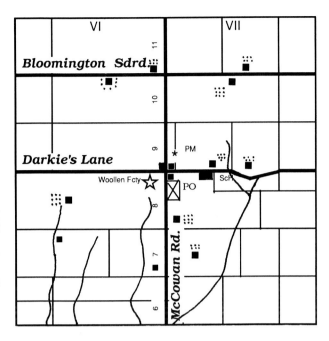

Lemonville, the quaint little community south of the Bloomington Sideroad on McCowan Road (the seventh concession road), was named for George Lemon, who received his grant of land on September 19, 1805, when he arrived from New York state. The village grew to be a thriving centre for local artisans and businesses until 1871, when the Toronto and Nipissing Railway came to Stouffville, bypassing Lemonville.

Settlers began to arrive in the early 1800s. Names such as Baker, Barkey, Burkholder, Cook, Hastings, Lemon, Lloyd and Pipher appear on early maps of the area. By 1853 the growing community was served by two hotels, but in the same year, the ladies and gentlemen of Lemonville and surrounding neighbourhoods successfully petitioned for a by-law prohibiting the sale of "ardent spirits." A resolution was passed that there would be no licence issued within a 2-mile radius of Lemonville.

The 1871 *Canadian Dominion Directory* recorded the population of Lemonville as one hundred, with tri-weekly mail delivery to a post office that had opened in 1854. Among the industries and businesses listed were John and Joseph Barkey, cabinet makers, on lot 3, concession 7, a sawmill operated by John Burkholder on lot 4, concession 6 (west side of McCowan Road), and Henderson's boot and shoe factory at the corner of McCowan Road and the Bethesda Sideroad. East on the Bethesda Sideroad was Harry Patterson's carriage works. J.W. Kitely was the operator of a woollen mill, and William White had a shoe repair shop across the road. One of the many storekeepers and postmasters was Adam Hastings, who was postmaster from 1870 to 1873.

The lane that runs east past the present-day Community Centre (originally S.S. #9) is known as Darkie's Lane. Originally it extended from Kennedy Road (the sixth concession road) through to the ninth concession road and formed the centre of the business community of Lemonville. Apparently the lane received its unusual name because of the abundance of trees that overhung the roadway, causing it to be extremely dark. Two sawmills were located on this road, as well as a grist mill that was in operation across from the schoolhouse. A hotel was situated on the corner, with J. Sutton as tavern keeper. George McKay (blacksmith), John P. Davis (carpenter), Samuel Gilbert (stone mason), James Hill (weaver), and Henry Winterstein (tanner) were just some of the numerous artisans working in the area.

ABOVE: Lemonville. Lynne Rubbens
BELOW: William Andrew Cook home, lot 14, concession 7.
Whitchurch-Stouffville Museum

The present Lemonville United church was built in 1856 as a Primitive Methodist Church with ground being reserved from the Pipher farm (lot 9, concession 7) for a cemetery. By 1920 it was one of a five-point charge, which meant it shared its minister with four other Methodist churches; however, by 1950, the once-large congregation had dwindled so badly that the church was closed and the building was used by the Dutch Reform Church for several years.

JAMES HASTINGS,
Manufacturer of
DOMINION GRAPE WINE.
Received Two Medals, Two Diplomas and Two Certificates from the Philadelphia Exhibition, 1876, for the best wine on exhibition.
Sold Wholesale and Retail at his residence, Lot 5, Con. 5, Whitchurch.
LEMONVILLE P. O.

ABOVE: Lemonville store
RIGHT: Kitely home, part lot 8, concession 6.
Whitchurch-Stouffville Museum

Macklem home, lot 8, concession 6.
Whitchurch-Stouffville Museum

In 1961 a new United Church congregation was formed, and services resumed in the little white church. The parsonage was located at the intersection of Darkie's Lane after 1893.

The schoolhouse (S.S. #9) that fronts on Darkie's Lane just east of McCowan Road was built in 1923 and enlarged in 1959. A log schoolhouse is reported to have been in use in Lemonville as early as 1813, and the 1885 Inspector's Report records "a frame house enlarged some years ago and supplied with modern desks and seats, the teacher Alexander Marshall Hannah—attendance 25." In 1972, with children being transported to larger area schools, the schoolhouse was sold and is now used as the Lemonville Community Centre.

Lemonville has long been known for the number of artesian wells in the area. In 1901 and again in 1908, companies were formed with plans to divert and pipe water to the south. Both schemes were defeated in the Ontario legislature.

Several well-known figures came from the Lemonville area, including Charles Hastings (1858 – 1931) who, as medical officer of health for the City of Toronto during the years 1910 to 1931, introduced enforced pasteurization of milk in 1911 and compulsory smallpox vaccinations in 1919, thus dramatically reducing the number of deaths from typhoid and smallpox.

New homes have been built all through the area. Farms have been sold for residential use, so few working farms remain. Two golf courses have opened, and McCowan Road has become a busy thoroughfare. Buildings that once served as stores, schools, or shops can still be discerned between the estate homes that replace the more modest farmhouses of the original settlers. As former city dwellers discover the charm of country life, the area is changing. Would Isaac, Jacob, or George Lemon recognize their home village if they were to return today?

SELDOM SEEN

Should you bring this name into conversation, someone is sure to say, "Where is that?" To locate Seldom Seen, turn north on McCowan Road (the seventh concession road) from the Aurora Sideroad. Continue for about 1 1/2 miles before coming to a deep gully and the end of the road! This is the community of Seldom Seen.

No one lived in this area until the late 1860s. The land still had to be cleared of the first virgin pine, and the sawmill owners of that day were also the land speculators. Robert McCormick, John Van Nostrand, and David Richardson, all operators of sawmills at that time, were property owners in the neighbourhood.

David Richardson's son George set up a mill on the east 100 acres of lot 25, concession 6, in 1869. He was the first to use the name Seldom Seen to explain where he and his family had relocated from their home in present-day Vandorf. George had been employed previously at the Van Nostrand Mills and had the experience needed to clear the wooded area that had been recently purchased by his father.

George operated the sawmill for four years, then the bush area was left to natural growth and was a source of firewood for family members for many years.

Adjacent lands were mostly pasture. A few new settlers came after the First World War. A branch of the Grand Trunk Railway ran through the land in concession 7 to Vivian Station and on to Sutton in Georgina Township. One of the railroad maps describes this area as Seldom Seen.

This line was discontinued about 1926, but the Whitchurch Highland Railroad Club, in co-operation with the Richmond Hill Steamers, operates small steam locomotives in the Seldom Seen area each weekend during summer months.

There is still no exit north from the corner of the St. John Sideroad and McCowan Road because the deep ravine is still a problem. Homes are built on each side, with entry either through Faulkner Avenue on the south or Cherry Street from the north. Seldom Seen remains seldom seen.

Seldom Seen
Lynne Rubbens

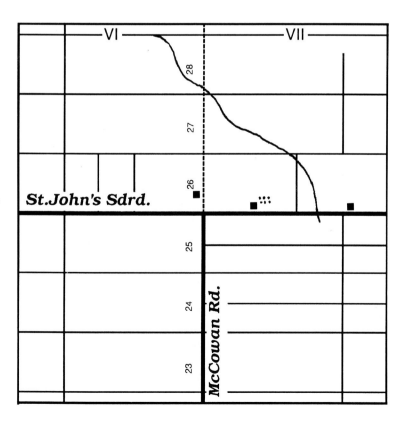

SHRUBMOUNT

As settlement spread eastward from Yonge Street during the mid-1800s, numerous small hamlets developed. These communities served as collection centres for the surrounding farming areas and usually offered services such as a post office, church, school, and store. They were usually situated at the intersection of a main road or near a water source (which was used to power local mills). "Following the survey of Upper Canada, roads were of first importance followed (almost simultaneously) by taverns and inns, places of accommodation for the traveller and his horse."

Such may have been the case with Shrubmount at the intersection of Davis Drive and McCowan Road (the seventh concession road). The origin of the name is unknown, but there was originally a hotel on the northwest corner of this intersection. According to the 1878 *Illustrated Historical Atlas of the County of York*, this property was registered to Mrs. Jonathan Paisley (lot 1, concession 7, East Gwillimbury). Between 1802 and 1809 patentees in the area included Abraham McDonald and George Althouse.

Within a period of approximately eight years, a post office was established in 1884 in the home of Francis Boake (lot 35, concession 6); a school (possibly an earlier Mennonite church) at the southwest corner of Davis Drive and McCowan Road, and a Methodist church, dedicated in 1877, formed the nucleus of this small rural community.

The post office that closed in 1888 was reopened in 1890, with Thomas Doyle serving as postmaster. Its existence was short-lived, however, and postal records show that it closed again in 1892.

There is no record of a schoolhouse in this area on the 1860 Tremaine map; however, the 1878 *Historical Atlas* shows a schoolhouse (on the east side of lot 35, concession 6) fronting on McCowan Road (the seventh concession road). There is some confusion whether this building was originally built as a Mennonite church or as a school (about 1882), but it appears that this building or another on the same site was used for a school until 1954 when a new building was erected on the same lot but fronting on Davis Drive. This was a union school with East Gwillimbury Township. Both buildings still stand. Following the creation of the York Region Board of Education in 1969–70, the building was sold and is now maintained as a private residence. Miss Jennie Larmon taught at Shrubmount school in 1890.

Shrubmount's speedy demise may be attributed to the fact that it was situated midway between two railway lines that served the northern and northwestern parts of Ontario (passing through Newmarket and Mount Albert); the land was light and sandy and therefore not conducive to good farming, and by the third quarter

Shrubmount
Lynne Rubbens

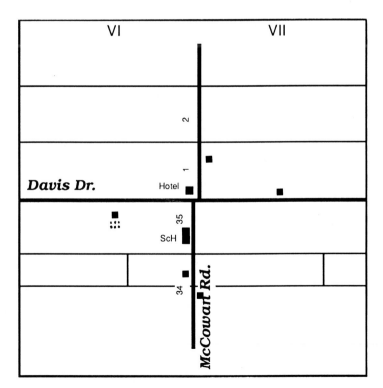

of the nineteenth century, this area of Whitchurch Township had been stripped of its forests by the lumbering magnates, creating a wasteland of blowing sand and unproductive soil.

In the early 1920s reforestation was introduced to the area, and one can still see the tree plantations that have been instrumental in helping to reclaim the land. These plantations are part of the Vivian Forest.

Davis Drive was paved in 1977, and in the late 1980s the intersection of Davis Drive and Highway 48 (the eighth concession road) was again improved and traffic lights were installed. On the north side of Davis Drive just west of the intersection one can still see the narrow gauge railway bed of the Lake Simcoe Junction Railway, which ran from Stouffville to Jackson's Point on Lake Simcoe from 1877 to 1927.

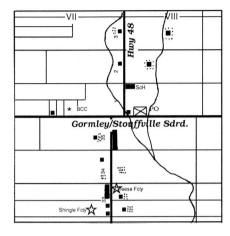

Ringwood
Lynne Rubbens

RINGWOOD

Ringwood, nicknamed Circle City by residents, was settled by the Fockler family in the late 1790s. Located at the intersection of the Stouffville Sideroad (the Markham-Stouffville town line) and Highway 48 (the eighth concession road), the hamlet was originally divided between two municipalities, Markham and Whitchurch.

George Fockler brought his family from Pennsylvania, settling 200 acres from the present highway to McCowan Road (the seventh concession road). By 1809 the Focklers had built a home on the northwest corner of the crossroads, and to the east Sam Fockler, George's son, built a hotel called Revere House. It was demolished for the widening of the highway in the early 1950s.

Ludwig Wideman and his parents were also early settlers of Ringwood. They arrived at lot 35, concession 8, Markham, in 1805, and their home, a white house east on the Stouffville Sideroad, still stands in 1993. In the uprising at Montgomery's Tavern, on Yonge Street just north of Eglinton Avenue, in the Rebellion of 1837, rebel Ludwig Wideman was one of the

fatalities. His son, Philip, continued farming and opened a marble works in the hamlet. He later moved his business to Stouffville.

George Sylvester built a general store in the early 1800s. Sylvester, the postmaster and general merchant, named the hamlet Ringwood in 1856, after a village of the same name in England from which he emigrated.

REVERE HOUSE,
RINGWOOD.

is one of the best Hotels in the county.   It is on the square all the time.

CHAS. FISHER, Proprietor.

Revere House hotel built by Sam Fockler.
Whitchurch-Stouffville Museum

Other early business included Jacob Brownsberger's harness shop and George Fockler's blacksmith's shop, where George Brownsberger shod oxen and horses and was famous for making copper ladles and betty lamps, which used fat for fuel. Abraham Grove operated a cheese factory, and Jacob Grove owned a shingle factory. McPherson Carriage and Wagon Works was on the east side of Highway 48, south of the Stouffville Sideroad. Abraham Lehman owned a carriage shop, as well as a store with his brother, Ludwig. Sam Lehman operated a lumber company on part of lot 3, concession 7. Sam Raymond operated another blacksmith's shop and was the inventor of a knotter, a binder part that knotted twine around grain sheaves, later patented by the Massey-Ferguson firm in one of its earlier incarnations and used on binders.

Newbury Button built a hotel called Ontario House in 1868 on the southwest corner of the crossroads. It operated until the 1920s. The large building was later changed to a snack bar, then a store, with numerous owners. It was demolished in 1986 to make way for the service station and snack bar now on the site.

A cluster of houses south on Highway 48 became known as Slabtown because of the piles of slab wood used for fuel in front of John Moyer's home. He sold the slabs, but for his livelihood he wove carpets.

Hammett's Holm was the name given to the southwest corner of Stouffville and McCowan roads, west of Ringwood. It was a tiny German community consisting of a store and post office, school classes held in a home (where students spoke only German), a cemetery, and possibly a church. In the late 1920s the cemetery stones were moved to other cemeteries when the land changed ownership. Nothing remains today to the mark the community.

The Ringwood Christian Church is one of the sisterhood of churches in Whitchurch Township. Built in 1868, the church still stands in 1993, west of the four corners on the north side of the Stouffville Sideroad.

TOP: *Harry Spang's harness shop, c. 1900.*   MIDDLE: *Ringwood.*
BOTTOM: *General store, north side of Stouffville/Gormley Sideroad, west of Highway 48.* Whitchurch-Stouffville Museum

A frame schoolhouse was built on Christian Lehman's property, lot 1, concession 8, and was later replaced by a new brick building, constructed in 1887. The school was known as Union School Section # 2, shared between Markham and Whitchurch students. It was closed in 1969 or 1970 and became a church meeting house for Bethel Assembly of God in 1972.

The Breuls, Mertens, Bartholomews, Grieves, Doughertys, Musselmans, Stouffers, and Mitchells were other early families in Ringwood's history. Norman Jones settled on lot 3, concession 8, in 1821, building a stone house that still stands on the east side of Highway 48, north of the Stouffville Sideroad.

In the mid-1940s, George Rodanz bought six farms that surrounded the four corners on the west side of the highway, known as Ringwood Farms. He was president of the Royal Winter Fair in Toronto and known worldwide as a breeder of Hereford cattle.

Fockler descendants have lived on the lands settled by their ancestors since 1797, but the community has changed drastically since they arrived two centuries ago. Buildings were knocked down to make way for improvements to Highway 48 in 1950. Although quite a number of early homes remain, industry is becoming the major focus of the community. Commercial and industrial condominiums were built in the 1980s and 1990s east on the Stouffville Sideroad. In 1857 the community's population was 200. The figure dropped to 124 by 1972.

BAKER HILL

On the west side of Highway 48 (the eighth concession road), just south of the Bloomington Sideroad, stands a white frame building, Baker Hill Baptist Church. Since its erection in 1867, on land purchased from Jacob Baker's farm (lot 8, concession 7), this church has been a place of worship for families who settled in the neighbourhood.

Several families by the name of Baker (all descendants of Jacob Becker, born in 1731 in Germany, and his wife, Anna Marie Brecht) immigrated to America and settled in Somerset County, Pennsylvania. About 1800 they decided to move to Canada as a family group, including children and grandchildren. Jacob somehow became lost on the way, and his wife waited at Niagara for two years in the futile hope that he would appear, before joining her family in York County. The family Bible records thirteen children in the family of Jacob and Anna Marie.

Three of the Baker sons settled and cleared land in the seventh concession of Whitchurch Township. In 1802 John Baker received a Crown grant of 200 acres at lot 7. Jacob Baker at

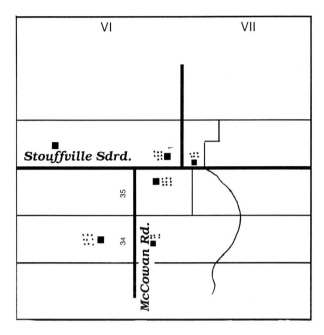

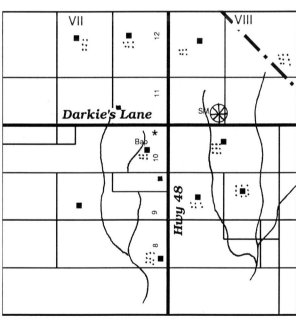

ABOVE: *Hammett's Holm*
BELOW: *Baker Hill*
Lynne Rubbens

ABOVE: ***Baker Hill Baptist Church***
RIGHT: ***Baker farmhouse***
Whitchurch-Stouffville Museum

a later date received 100 acres, the east half of lot 8, and Emanuel Baker in 1815 purchased from Isaac Davis the east half of lot 9, 100 acres. John Baker also owned lots 9 and 10 in the eighth concession, where he established and operated a sawmill.

The small community was composed of members of the Baptist faith. During the first half of the nineteenth century, they were compelled to travel many miles to the Second Markham Baptist Church, at that time known as Providence Church, on the Stouffville Sideroad (now Springvale Baptist Church). Road conditions were so poor that churchgoers had to walk or ride horseback. As a result, only the strong and younger members of the community could attend Sunday service, leaving children and grandparents at home. After much thought and prayer, the community decided that a chapel should be built at Baker Hill. Jacob Baker sold a portion of lot 8 to Joel Baker and other trustees for the use of the congregation of Baptists. The deed was dated April 15, 1867. During the previous week, Joel Baker had sold a parcel of land from his lot 9 to Jacob Baker and other trustees to be used as a cemetery. These lots were separated by Darkie's Lane, the long road in the middle of the township block. Children travelled this road west to school at Lemonville.

Preaching began in the new chapel on March 24, 1867, morning and evening, to alternate with service at the Second Markham Baptist Church every other sabbath. The arrangement continued until 1923, when the Baker Hill members organized the Baker Hill Regular Baptist

Church. In 1953 they joined the Fellowship Evangelical Baptist Churches of Canada. Family names of those attending the early church included Baker, Walker, Jamieson, Musselman, Fockler, Pipher, Henderson, Hashell, Jackman, and Lemon. Many of the preachers who served Baker Hill and Second Markham Baptist churches were students from the University of Toronto. They were entertained for the weekend in the homes of the church members. In later years there were permanent ordained ministers.

Music was an important to Baker family life, and their keen interest was reflected in the children's singing school and in the excellent choirs that originated at the church.

Several members of the Baker family have held seats in local and provincial governments over the years, adding to the contributions of this family to the community.

Today the Baker Hill Baptist Church remains the focal point of the tiny community.

BALLANTRAE

Although Vivian was considered to be the centre of the Whitchurch lumbering industry, mainly because of the influence and holdings of the McCormick family, it was Ballantrae, lying approximately 2½ miles south at the intersection of the Aurora Sideroad and Highway 48 (the eighth concession road) that developed into an economic centre to service the industry. Ballantrae was settled in the early 1800s, its population gradually increasing to approximately 100 by 1860 and 300 by 1895. The name is thought to have originated in Ireland, as many local settlers had emigrated from there.

Ballantrae
Lynne Rubbens

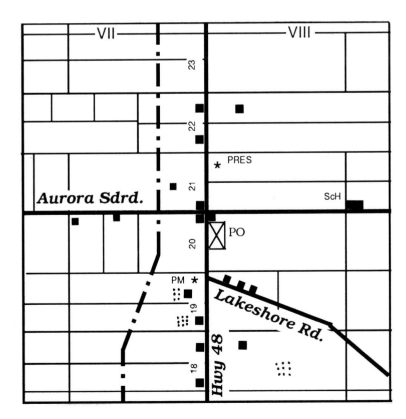

According to the York Census of 1851, Ballantrae was beginning to emerge as a busy service centre for the surrounding rural area. Edward McMillan's inn and a hotel operated by William Galloway were among the first commercial enterprises in the hamlet. By 1860 many inns were to be found in the immediate area. James Lever sold one acre of land on the southwest side of the four corners (lot 20, concession 7 east) to Robert McCordock in 1858. McCordock built a general store on the property, and so began the hamlet of Ballantrae. The following year the property was sold to James DeGeer, who became the first postmaster. Within ten years Lorenzo Badgerow had sold land to Edward Gray, a shoemaker (lot 20, concession 8 southwest). William Reynolds established a blacksmith's shop on the west side of Highway 48, just south of the four corners. Richard L. Macey opened a general store on the southeast corner of the intersection, and Daniel Prior was listed in the 1871 York

Census as storekeeper and postmaster (lot 20, concession 8) with mail being delivered three times a week. In 1870 Robert Hill, a carpenter by trade, opened a general store in the hamlet (lot 19, concession 8) which he ran until 1896, when he built a new one. Early council meetings were frequently held in Hill's hall. Hill was born in Whitchurch in 1833.

Another early settler listed in the 1861 Whitchurch Census was Elijah Miller (lot 20, concession 8), who ran a store and inn and later a hotel until about 1881, when he moved to Stouffville and established the Mansion Hotel. James Wright also owned a hotel in the hamlet about the same time, although the exact location is unknown.

On the east side of Highway 48, north of the intersection, Messrs. Hood and Davies opened a blacksmith's shop and the Mayflower Stamping Company, established in 1889 on the Hood property (lot 22, concession 8 west). The individualized stamps were used to mark barrels and containers.

Ballantrae was on the edge of the vast lumbering industry centred in Vivian, having four or five of the many sawmills operating in the vicinity. This, along with the construction of the Lake Simcoe Junction Railway, a spur line of the Toronto and Nipissing Railway, built in 1877, running from Stouffville north to Jackson's Point on Lake Simcoe, certainly bolstered its economic growth and ensured stability for a number of years. The "Mary Ann" or "Grandma's Trunk," as it was affectionately called, passed through Ballantrae just west of the intersection of Highway 48 with the Aurora Sideroad. The line carried both freight and passengers, and the trip to Lake Simcoe was a popular day excursion. On the northbound trip from Stouffville, local inhabitants say that if the engineer did not gain enough momentum while crossing the Bloomington Road and on north to Ballantrae, the engine would be forced

Work on Lake Simcoe Junction Railway tool shed c. 1925. Left: Dan Baker, section foreman. Centre: Hec Pollard. Markham District Historical Museum

to back up and try again, especially if the tracks were slippery. Many a time the engineer had to leave one section of the train at the bottom of the grade while he continued on to Ballantrae, returning for the remaining section.

The line was an important link to the lumbering industry and the town because roads in the area were hazardous at the best of times. Corduroy roads were in constant need of attention, and before the highway was diverted in the early 1940s the area just south of Ballantrae was especially troublesome. The road ran straight over Mud Lake, not a true lake but a very swampy area, and the story is often told of days spent filling the area with gravel to support the floating road, only to have it disappear during the night.

Two churches were established within the limits of the community. The 1878 *Illustrated Historical Atlas of the County of York* shows the locations of a Presbyterian church, north of the four corners on the east side of Highway 48, and the Ballantrae Methodist Church, on the west side of the highway (lot 19, concession 7 east). In 1939 a fire destroyed the church and shed, but the contents were saved. A new church was built on the foundations and is still in use as St. Georgio Orthodox Church. The Presbyterian church was moved from the hamlet to Musselman's Lake in 1924.

By 1878 the *Historical Atlas* shows a schoolhouse on the present site at lot 21, concession 8, the north side of the Aurora Sideroad. The property was owned by George Quantz, who was paid the sum of $25 in 1881 for the purchase of one-half acre by trustees who erected a school in 1884. By the following year, the enrolment totalled about forty pupils, and they were taught by Edwin Ball. In 1935 another school was built and subsequently destroyed by fire in 1973. A modern building has since been erected on the site to accommodate approximately 450 students.

With the demise of the lumbering and farming industries in the area, due largely to erosion and overuse, Ballantrae never reached its full potential. Population declined dramatically about the turn of the century as roads improved and people travelled to the larger towns springing up around the railways.

Improvements to Highway 48 in the 1940s and '50s caused major changes to the four corners of Ballantrae. Many of the stores and the hotel on the southeast corner disappeared.

TOP LEFT: *Ballantrae Methodist Church*
BOTTOM LEFT: *Ballantrae Public School S.S. #11*
RIGHT: *Hotel and general store, Ballantrae.*
Whitchurch-Stouffville Museum

In the 1970s further road work was done, and the remaining general store, the hotel, and a service station on the southwest corner were demolished. South of Lake Road on the east side of the highway, Radford's store and garage were replaced by a new restaurant and variety store.

A new three-hundred-unit subdivision was built in the early 1970s southwest of the intersection, and a strip mall was added to the south entrance road. There are now a number of service stations, a seasonal garden centre, and two more housing complexes within the boundaries of the hamlet.

The Whitchurch Centennial Centre, built in 1967–68, just west of the school, is surrounded by a park containing a baseball diamond, tennis courts, play areas, and a thriving seniors' centre.

Descendants of some of the first families in the area still reside in the community. A grand red-and-cream-brick house, built in 1870 on the east side of Highway 48, is one of the few remaining homes belonging to the once-thriving hamlet of Ballantrae.

VIVIAN

This tiny community, first known as Sexsmith's Corners, was situated at the intersection of Highway 48 (the 8th concession road) and the Vivian Sideroad.

By 1803 most of the land in this area had been divided among early patentees, including John Cornwell (lot 31), Samuel Betzner (lot 29), Jacob Bechtel, Sr. (lot 30), and Adam Cline (lot 32). These men merely cleared and sold the land rather than settling it.

Vivian
Lynne Rubbens

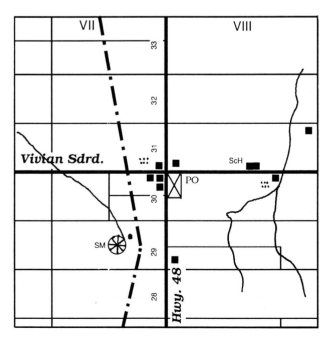

Early settlers in the area, seeing the virgin stands of giant white pine, were confident that the land would support farming and the area would become a centre of extensive lumbering operations in the latter half of the nineteenth century. Much of the pine was used by the Royal Navy as masts and most of the lumber was exported to England in accordance with the White Pine Clause in early land grants. The law was difficult to enforce, and a lucrative lumbering industry developed in part by Robert McCormick, flourished throughout the nineteenth century. By 1900 the local lumber industry had become a victim of its own success. The great pine forests had been destroyed, and by 1920 the land around this area of Whitchurch resembled a desert.

In December 1866 a post office was established, making Vivian the official name of the hamlet. George Sexsmith, the first postmaster, (1866–1867) also ran a local general store and hotel. In December 1867 election nominations were held at Sexsmith Hall. The post office operated for 64 years, with only five postmasters.

Early in Vivian's history Jonathan Randall ran a wayside inn and shingle mill on the southwest corner of the intersection (lot 30, concession 7 east), and Robert Heasty (Hasty) operated a steam sawmill (lot 29, concession 7

McCormick general store, built in 1883 at Vivian.
Whitchurch-Stouffville Museum

east) in partnership with Robert McCormick. The 1871 Whitchurch Census lists Jacob Rose as shingle maker (lot 29, concession 8).

The name Robert McCormick was synonymous with lumbering in the area. The family settled there in 1866, and by 1868 McCormick was firmly established as a sawyer. The 1878 *Historical Atlas* includes an illustration of his business card: "McCormick & Sons, General Store—dealers and manufacturers in lumber, lath, shingles, beading, hoops." Large tracts of land held by the McCormick family were systematically stripped of their timber in a relatively short period of time (approximately 35 years). Up to fifteen sawmills operated in the area.

With the sawmill and shingle factory (lot 29, concession 7 east), the family owned and operated a general store, a blacksmith's shop, a maple sugar bush to the southeast of the four corners (later owned and operated by Ratcliff Lumber), and early editions of the *Newmarket Era* report plans for a chopping mill and an oatmeal mill.

> ROBT. McCORMICK & SONS,
> # GENERAL STORE KEEPERS,
> *At the Vivian Post Office, Whitchurch.*
> ALSO MANUFACTURERS & DEALERS IN
> ## LUMBER, LATH, SHINGLES, HEADING, HOOPS.
> A Speciality in patent machine made hoops, four of which are equal to ten of the ordinary.

The Green Bush Hotel, on the southwest side of the four corners, was the centre of social life in the small community. At times more than one hundred buggies would be tied up outside. This hotel was also a halfway house for travellers from Lake Simcoe to Toronto.

Influencing the commercial evolution of Vivian was the fact that McCormick and other sawmill owners in the area had successfully lobbied for a station on the Lake Simcoe Junction Railway that ran from Stouffville to Jackson's Point. The line was constructed in 1877, with as many as four hundred men working in the Vivian area. The station was on the north side of the Vivian Sideroad west of Highway 48 and was a waiting room and sectionhouse combined. The sectionhouse was the accommodation provided for a section man or foreman, who was the railway employee responsible for maintaining a section of track. Just south of Cherry Street ran a spur line, to the east, for hauling fine sand to be used in the locomotive sanders.

ABOVE: *Robert McCormick home, built in 1881, destroyed by fire.*
BELOW: *McCormick Memorial Church*
Whitchurch-Stouffville Museum

The original station burnt down in 1919 under tragic circumstances. The son of the sectionman had been drowned the day before, and in preparation for his funeral reception a coal-oil stove had tipped over, setting fire to the freight shed. In minutes the building was gone and the intense heat warped the rails in front of the station. The station was rebuilt in 1920, but the Lake Simcoe Junction Railway line was abandoned in 1927.

In 1881 Robert McCormick built an elegant home on the northwest corner of the Vivian Sideroad and Highway 48 (lot 31, concession 7). The red-brick building consisted of nineteen rooms and was resplendent with large verandahs and balconies. A beautiful wrought-iron fence surrounded it, separating the grounds from the roadside. This wonderful mansion was destroyed by fire in 1971, having lain derelict for years.

In 1883 a second building, the McCormick General Store, was constructed on the southeast corner of the intersection (lot 30, concession 8), after the original post office and hotel structure was destroyed by an arsonist in the same year. The building still stands and is now a private residence.

Vivian School, S.S. #5, is on the north side of the Vivian Sideroad (lot 31, concession 8). According to records at the Ontario Archives, the original log schoolhouse on the Seth Willson property had thirteen students in 1850. In 1873 McCormick and his wife deeded a half acre of land at lot 31 to trustees of S.S. #5. The new frame schoolhouse was built to the west of the stream, and by 1885 attendance had risen to forty pupils. A Miss A. Myers was one of the early teachers at the school.

A new two-room brick school was built in 1955, closer to Highway 48, but with the establishment of the Regional Board of Education in 1971, rural schools were closed and Vivian School was sold. It was subsequently used as the Vivian Outdoor Education Centre (run through York Region Board of Education), primarily owing to its proximity to the Vivian Forest.

Church services for local inhabitants were held at McCormick's store and prior to that in the Shrubmount school (lot 35, concession 6 east). In 1938 services were held in the old Green Bush Hotel, which was subsequently demolished, while construction on the McCormick Memorial Church was begun. The congregation was affiliated with the Baptist Church.

Unfortunately as the forest disappeared so did the light topsoil. Pockets of blowsand developed and began to advance across crop land in the area. In 1910 York County Council adopted a plan of reforestation, but it was not until 1920 that a committee was formed and York County started to replant in 1924 on lot 28, concession 8.

In 1950 the Vivian Forest, established as a recreation and educational area, was made a Crown Game Reserve. Through careful study and continued planting, the forest now affords opportunities for many outdoor activities throughout the year, providing an oasis of calm in an increasingly urban environment.

Hartman
Lynne Rubbens

HARTMAN

The hamlet of Hartman was at the crossroads of Davis Drive and the 9th concession road (Ninth Line).

Hartman was named in honour of Joseph H. Hartman, although he did not actually live in the community. Hartman, born in 1821, was the son of John and Mary Hartman, who had immigrated to Canada from Pennsylvania with many other Quaker settlers in 1808. He began his career as a teacher in a small log schoolhouse near his home, and he rapidly rose to prominence in local affairs. A Temperance supporter and radical reformer, Hartman was also a leader in the Methodist Connexion, was first reeve of Whitchurch (1850–1859), and a warden of York County for six terms (1853–1859). His 200-acre farm was at Leslie Avenue and the Aurora Sideroad (lot 20, concession 2). Hartman died at the youthful age of thirty-eight and is buried in Aurora.

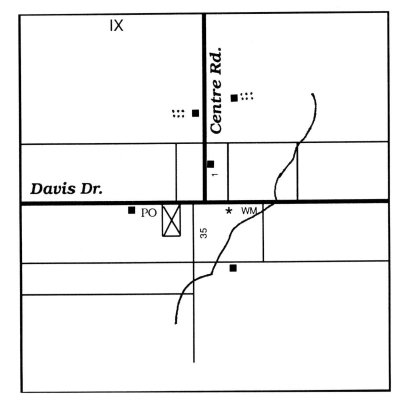

The earliest Crown grants in the area were issued, beginning in 1803, to Samuel Bricker (lot 34, concession 8), Philip Saltberger (lot 35, concession 8), and Benham Preston (lots 32–35, concession 9). Along with seven other families of the Mennonite faith, these settlers took land grants in Whitchurch Township because they were having difficulty obtaining clear deeds for land they had hoped to buy in Waterloo County near Kitchener, Ontario. Bricker was able to borrow enough money from relatives in Pennsylvania to form a joint stock company known as the German Company, and this enabled the families to buy the land in Waterloo County. Eight of these families merely cleared the land in Whitchurch, as required, and sold the acreage within a few years. Samuel Bricker, however, held the property until 1847, when he sold the east half to William Graham. In 1852 he sold the remaining west half of his land to John Grose, whose descendants are still there.

Hartman Methodist Church
Whitchurch-Stouffville Museum

Primarily a farming community, the hamlet did acquire a post office, one of the earliest in York County, which opened in 1863 under its first postmaster, David Terry. He was succeeded by Hugh Campbell (lot 35, concession 8) and after his death by Mrs. Campbell. The mail was processed weekly. The post office was closed in 1884 as the hamlet decreased in size and vitality when larger neighbouring towns emerged.

The Canada Directory of 1869 lists two blacksmiths (Stephen Lefraugh, Hugh Graham), two carpenters (Albert Rose, George Thirsk), a postmaster, and several farmers as inhabitants of the tiny community.

According to the 1878 *Illustrated Historical Atlas of the County of York*, early landowners included William Sawdon, John Graham, James Grose, and Allen and Benjamin Graham.

The Grahams emigrated with their parents from Yorkshire, England, in 1842. The family, spinners and weavers by trade, were unaccustomed to farm life and found settling the land unnaturally severe. By the 1860s they had acquired approximately 1400 acres of land in different areas of York County. After the death of their father in 1860, Allen and Benjamin formed a partnership combining farming and wool manufacturing, which lasted for some years. Allen held approximately 640 acres on the north side of Davis Drive (lots 1 and 2, concession 8, East Gwillimbury), and 80 acres on the south side of Davis Drive (part of lots 34 and 35, concession 8 Whitchurch). Benjamin retained the remaining acreage.

A log schoolhouse was on the property of Isaac Rose (lot 1, concession 8, East Gwillimbury), who had purchased his land from Ralph and James Smalley in 1858. Isaac Rose, a United Empire Loyalist of Dutch descent, had immigrated to the area from Pennsylvania. A consolidation of educational facilities resulted in the building of a union school, U.S.S. #11 (Scott Township) in 1915, on the northeast corner of Davis Drive and Regional Road 30, the convergence of four townships. The school was closed in 1967, but the building still stands in 1993 and is now a private residence. The log schoolhouse was also used for church services in the early days of the community. In 1863 a Primitive Methodist church was built on the Whitchurch side of Davis Drive on land donated by Allen Graham. A union of all Methodist churches took place in 1883, and the Hartman church became Wesleyan Methodist. Eight years later George Haigh added two small parcels of land to the western and southern borders of the church property, and the church sheds were erected along the western boundary. Again in 1899 property was added to the south side, and a new church was erected on the foundations of the older building, which was subsequently sold, a part of it being used as an outbuilding on the Albert Howlett farm nearby. The new church was named Hartman Methodist Church. At the time of Church Union in 1925, Hartman Methodist became Hartman United under the ministry of Rev. H. Hutcheson. In 1967 the church closed owing to insufficient congregants, and in the following year the building was sold to a private owner.

All that remains to mark the site of the little community of Hartman is the cemetery on the south side of Davis Drive, just east of Highway 48 (the gates were erected through the contributions of many local inhabitants), and the former church building.

STOUFFVILLE

Abraham Stouffer, a Pennsylvanian miller, brought his business to Canada in the early 1800s, giving his name to Stouffville, the most southeastern community in Whitchurch Township.

The first Stouffers arrived in the United States in 1709 from Switzerland. In the fall of 1804 the descendants, travelling in covered wagons, made the journey to Canada from Chambersburg, Pennsylvania. They settled on 600 acres at Main and Mill streets on the Markham-Stouffville town line (lot 35, Markham, and lots 1 and 2, concession 9 Whitchurch), the present-day site of the Whitchurch-Stouffville Public Library.

Stouffer built several mills between 1817 and 1824. A grist mill was built at the present-day corner of Market and Main streets. Two mills burned down at this site before a new mill was built on the north side of the street, a little to the west. He also built a sawmill on the old site.

The community began to take shape when a general store was opened in a corner of the grist mill operated by Charles Sheldon. A blacksmith's shop and tavern were built next. Ben Boyer and his son, John, built a store, a drugstore, and later a post office. Charles Sheldon was appointed the first post-master in 1832.

Stouffville, based on Illustrated Historical Atlas of the County of York, *1878.*
Lynne Rubbens

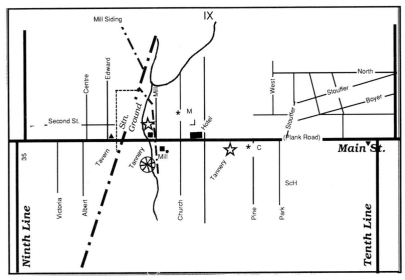

ABOVE: O'Brien Avenue looking north.
BELOW: Main Street, northwest corner of
Mill Street, Stouffville.
Whitchurch-Stouffville Museum

In the same year a log schoolhouse was built on the present site of the Stouffville United Church on Church Street. From 1841 the building was also used for Sunday Methodist church services. It was bought by the Methodists in 1865, renovated, and moved across the street in 1872, when a new church was built on the old site. After the Methodist purchase, classes were held in the Orange Hall on Fockler Lane. This street was located behind the south-side Main Street stores, from Church Street west to Market Street.

Three small buildings on the site of the present Summitview Public School held classes until 1877. One was moved, the other converted to a home, and the last torn down to make room for a four-room brick schoolhouse. The school was then known as the Continuation School, serving students from Grades 1 to 11. The school burnt down in 1917, and a new one was erected the next year.

After several additions (including kindergarten and Form V or Grade 13), 10 acres of land were purchased on Edward Street in 1954 and Stouffville District Secondary School was erected. Orchard Park Public School was built in the mid-1950s when Summitview became overcrowded. St. Mark Catholic School was built at Glad Park and Elm roads in 1965 for elementary students.

In a diary Henry Van Der Smisson, who came to Stouffville from England in 1839 and worked in a store and distillery on Market Street, wrote that the village had no church, baker, or butcher, and life was not easy. He noted, however, that saddlebag preachers sometimes arrived and held meetings in the schoolhouse.

In the 1830s Stouffville was the centre of the reform party in this area. At that time the village was centred near the mills on the Whitchurch side of the road.

In the early 1840s the neighbourhood was terrorized by a gang from Markham, leading to the formation of a criminal-justice committee, called the Society for the Apprehension of Felons. Most of the gang members lived in Markham, Pickering, Scarborough, Whitchurch, and Uxbridge townships, were descendants of the early settlers, owned some property and were outwardly respectable. They tried to protect themselves by blackmailing possible witnesses, but a number were still brought to trial in 1846 for burglary, robbery with violence, forgery and other larcenies. In the 1860s the Stouffville association won praise from a grand jury for bringing to justice a gang of horse thieves.

Stouffville grew rapidly in the 1840s. By 1846 Stouffville was a road village, centred along one road instead of around an intersection of two roads. The village had two taverns but little industry besides the mills.

In 1848 a Congregational church was built in the area of the cemetery. Rev. Kribbs, a Congregationalist, arrived to start a mission in the 1840s. The members worshipped in their first building for twenty-seven years before erecting a new one at the corner of Main and Stouffer streets. The church did the moral policing of the village. The area behind the old church was donated to the town for a municipal cemetery. The newer church stands today as the Memorial Christian Church. By the time the church was built, Stouffville had approximately 350 inhabitants.

Abraham Stouffer died in October 1851, and his son, Christian, sold the mills to Edward Wheler (Wheeler). By this time, lumbering, cabinet making, wagon making, and marble works existed, but the mills and Van Busack's harness shop seem to have been the most important enterprises in the fifties and early sixties.

Other industries were added in the late 1870s, including pump works, agricultural implements, a foundry, and a spring-bed factory. In the 1860s and 1870s stagecoach lines ran to Newmarket and Whitby, and to Markham and Uxbridge.

The building of the narrow-gauge Toronto and Nipissing Railway in 1871 was watched with a great deal of anticipation by the local business community who assumed that increased economic activity would follow the coming of the railway. In 1870 the population was approximately seven hundred and it was expected to double in ten years, but the hopes of the business people were not realized for many years. There were as many as ten hotels by 1880 along Stouffville Road from Highway 48 (the eighth concession road) to the town line (tenth concession road), including the Mansion House, which still stands today. Business increased when the spur-line Lake Simcoe Junction Railway was built from Stouffville north to Lake Simcoe in 1877. The built-up area extended some distance west of the railway. By 1901 the town's population had increased to 1,223.

Stouffville was then called Stouffville Junction. The railway brought profits to the mill owner Edward Wheler, who secured contracts for fencing and ties for that section. Engine sheds and water towers through to the Toronto and Nipissing's terminus at Coboconk, on Balsam Lake in the Kawarthas, were also included in his work.

The railway and population growth prompted many residents to consider separate municipal administration for the community. In January 1876 Wheler and others submitted a petition to York County Council for Stouffville's incorporation as a village. The by-law was

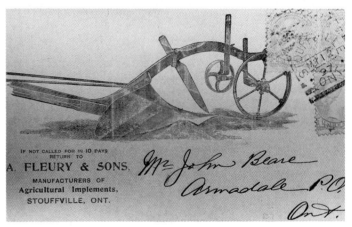

ABOVE: *Main Street, east of railway tracks, c. 1910.* Whitchurch-Stouffville Museum

BELOW: *Company in King, Aurora, Markham, Stouffville.* Russ Beare

*ABOVE LEFT: **Alexander Grubin, jewellery store, 1897.***
*ABOVE RIGHT: **Spofford's dry goods, corner of Main and Mill streets.***
*BELOW LEFT: **Nighswander paint shop, northwest corner of Baker Avenue and Main Street.***
*BELOW RIGHT: **Albert Street cider company, c. 1900.***
Whitchurch-Stouffville Museum

carried by council on February 4. The first Stouffville council met on January 15, 1877; James Dougherty, a Stouffville hardware merchant served, as its first reeve.

The village's first library was established in 1877. The prime promoter was J. Wideman, editor of the *Alert*, a local newspaper. In 1923 the Carnegie Library was built with a grant of $6,000 from the foundation and the generosity of local residents.

The decade of the 1880s witnessed a building boom especially west of the railway tracks. Rupert Avenue, Albert Street, and Victoria Street were surveyed into lots. New buildings were erected on Main Street and on Mill and Market streets.

Daley Hall was built at the southwest corner of Market and Main streets and was the pride of the village. It contained an ice surface for curling and skating, a farmer's market, a concert

Martin Tait's butcher shop, 6203 Main Street, Stouffville.
Whitchurch-Stouffville Museum

hall, and a special room for the town band. This building burnt down in 1923. Another concert hall was built in 1903. It became a movie theatre in 1923 and eventually became the Town of Whitchurch-Stouffville's municipal offices. In about 1927 a new federal post office was erected on Main Street. Another new post office was built in Stouffville's centennial year of 1977, as well as a new larger library.

In 1971 Stouffville united with part of Whitchurch Township, forming the Town of Whitchurch-Stouffville. Another boundary change for Stouffville in that year increased the community's size to include lots 34 to 32 Markham Township. The town received its coat of arms in 1973. It depicts a British Union banner of 1707, symbolizing the United Empire Loyalists who settled in the Markham section of the town, a white church to symbolize Whitchurch, and the star and chalice from the Stouffers' coat of arms to symbolize Stouffville. The crest at the top of the coat of arms is the dove of peace, the original seal of Whitchurch.

The first subdivision was built on former farmland in 1953, extending from Park Drive to Baker Avenue and north to Manitoba Street. Two huge commercial buildings became part of Stouffville on Main Street west of the Ninth Line (the ninth concession road). In 1971 Stouffville had a population of 5,036, a figure that has almost doubled in the past twenty years to approximately nine thousand in 1993.

Many historic homes remain in Stouffville, lining Main Street. While the town has grown commercially and in population, the spirit of its ancestors characterizes the small-town atmosphere of present-day Stouffville.

More detailed information on Stouffville's historical development can be found in *Stouffville: 1877–1977*, a pictorial history of the community.

BLOOMINGTON

The first landowners at Bloomington, at the corner of the Ninth Line (the ninth concession road) and the Bloomington Sideroad, never stayed long enough to put down roots in the new community.

The first land grantee, Ebenezer Jones, received 200 acres at the northwest corner (lot 11, concession 8) in 1804. Jones subsequently sold the land in 1815 to John McGill. The second settler, William Eadus, received 100 acres in 1812 on the southeast corner (part of lot 10, concession 9) and then sold the west part to Ezekiel Benson only fifteen days later.

Thomas Lundy also sold his 200 acres of granted land on the southwest corner (lot 10, concession 8) in 1820, after only five days of ownership, to Jonas Boyer. Boyer kept the land for twenty-two years and became a prominent citizen, serving as a magistrate for the Whitchurch district and later on, in 1846, as Stouffville's postmaster. The last quadrant of Bloomington, the northeast corner (lot 11, concession 9) was bought by John Hamilton in 1833.

Early settlers who stayed and farmed the lands of Bloomington and area were mainly Quakers, Mennonites, and United Empire Loyalists.

S. Patterson was the community's first postmaster from 1863 to 1870. Maxson Jones settled in the 1850s on lot 10, concession 9, the southeast corner of the intersecting roads. He was the community's second postmaster and is reputedly the man who registered the community's name in 1869, likely taking the name from a town of the same name in Illinois. Jones, who had emigrated from the United States, also served as a magistrate, storekeeper, and a holder of municipal offices, from assessor to reeve (the latter from 1882–85, and 1889–91)

*LEFT: **Bloomington.** Lynne Rubbens*
*RIGHT: **Bloomington school students,**
c. 1898.*
Whitchurch-Stouffville Museum

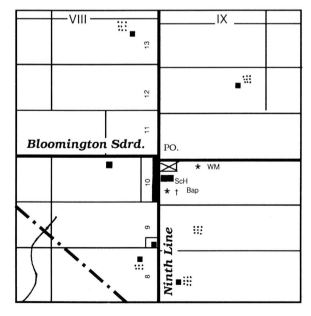

of Whitchurch Township. At the time of publication, the house he built still stands on the property and is used as a seniors' residence, Green Gables.

Industry in Bloomington in the nineteenth century included woodworking shops, where carriages and furniture were fashioned, blacksmith's shops, weavers, a chopping mill, a watch-repair shop, three sawmills within a short distance of the community, a photographic studio, a post office, and a general store. In 1893 the community's population was seventy-five (a figure that barely increased by 1966 to eighty-four). Part of the blacksmith's shop lives on as a portion of a present-day home, directly opposite the nursing home. The post office closed in 1920.

Earlier in the nineteenth century, a hotel may have operated out of a building that was still used as a home in 1993 on the northeast corner of the Ninth Line and the Bloomington Sideroad.

Maxson Jones home
Whitchurch-Stouffville Museum

The lumber industry, operated through the area sawmills, was once big business in Bloomington and the surrounding area. Transient French-Canadian lumber workers cut down the huge pine trees on the west side of concession 9 to create 100-foot high masts for British ships.

A log building on lot 10, concession 9 was likely the first schoolhouse in Bloomington. A new frame school was constructed in 1826 and a brick building built in 1898. Additions were made before the school was closed and sold to make way for the central school system created through regionalization in 1971. The schoolhouse is currently a private home.

BLOOMINGTON CHRISTIAN CHURCH was built in 1852 southeast of the crossroads. A cemetery was established to the north, its graves dating from 1832. The cemetery property was on land owned at the time by Robert Graham. By 1867 the church had 140 members, and in 1892 the present structure, still in use, was built across the road on the west side of the Ninth Line. In 1956 the church severed its connection with the Christian Conference and joined the Associated Gospel Churches of Ontario.

Bloomington Christian Church congregation.
Whitchurch-Stouffville Museum

Musselman's Lake
Lynne Rubbens

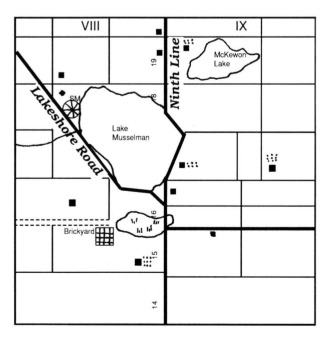

After years of meeting in the old log schoolhouse and in the Christian church, Bloomington Methodist Church was built in 1869 on Bloomington Road east of the Ninth Line. Services were held until 1939, when the church building was sold and moved to Buttonville, where it now serves as a community hall. The small Bloomington Methodist cemetery still lies on the south side of Bloomington Road, identified by a sign and fencing.

Bloomington once had its own community hall: its foundation was discovered on land across from the school.

Bloomington was home to farmers for many years, until recently when residential developments began to appear. Many farms remained in the same family for more than a century, including the Fairles farm, bought by Thomas Fairles in 1847, the Storry farm, bought by William Storry in 1820, the Tranmer farm, bought by Robert Tranmer in 1846, and the Lemon farm, bought by Jonathan Lemon in 1860.

MUSSELMAN'S LAKE

Musselman's Lake, a community that surrounds the lake of the same name, owes its existence to two events: the ice age and immigration of Pennsylvanians to the area.

The approximately 123-acre lake is located on the Oak Ridges moraine between Highway 48 (the eighth concession road) and the Ninth Line, and the Aurora and Bloomington sideroads. It has also been known as Lake

Musselman and Musselman Lake. It was formed during the ice age through glacial movement. Ice masses were buried and then melted to form kettle lakes connected by underground springs.

Some of the original settlers included Ronald McDonnell or McDonald, who received some 800 acres in the area, David Albertson, and William Harson. By 1878 these men were no longer associated with the area. Some other settlers given early land grants remained near the lake, including John Connor (part of lot 16, concession 8), Ambrose Noble (another part of lot 16, concession 8), the Helmkays (part of lot 17, concession 9) and the McKewons (part of lot 20, concession 9).

Other neighbours settled in the area by 1878 included Wismer, Hill, Laney, Miller, Reid, Pettet, Moore, Nesbitt, Gray, Urquhart, Appleton, and Farrier. Many of these early pioneers farmed the land around the lake.

The Musselmans, among the first families to come to the region from Pennsylvania in 1803, first settled on leased land in Vaughan. In 1807 members of the Musselman family purchased land in Whitchurch Township: William (lot 7, concession 7) in Lemonville, and Peter and Jacob (lot 18, concession 8) at what became Lake Musselman. Jacob's property was located on the west side of the lake.

By mid-century the lake was used as a source of water for a steam-driven sawmill located on Charles Appleton's property on lot 18, concession 8, on the northwest corner of the lake. The area was prime forest land when settlers arrived, but was eventually stripped clear like many other forested lands. A river once wound by the mill but was clogged with sawdust and eventually stopped running. The mill was listed under Appleton's name in the 1871 census as a steam sawmill that operated year-round. Appleton, originally from England, was something of an inventor. In 1889 he applied for a patent for a fire escape and had created a car-coupling and sleigh brake. He lived from 1823 to 1893 and is buried in Churchill cemetery beside his wife, Emily McPherson (1821–1873). His home still stands in 1993 on the north side of Lakeshore Road west of Byron Street.

An early map of the area shows a schoolhouse on the lake road at lot 19, concession 8. This log schoolhouse was evidently built in 1848 and used also for Sunday services. Teachers in the school were Jimmie Dougherty and Maxson Jones.

By 1860 the school had disappeared. It was not until 1864 that educational needs were again served when a school was built for the first time in nearby Ballantrae. Lake students still attend Ballantrae Public.

*ABOVE: **Farmland around Musselman's Lake.***

*BELOW: **Lakeshore Drive, 1910.***
Whitchurch-Stouffville Museum

ABOVE LEFT: View of Musselman's Lake
ABOVE RIGHT: Lakefront cottages
MIDDLE LEFT: Camping at Musselman's Lake, c. 1930.
MIDDLE RIGHT: Cedar Beach
RIGHT: Shadow Lake Camp when owned by Eaton's.
Whitchurch-Stouffville Museum

Although a majority of residents around the lake in the early years were farmers, other occupations are represented in the 1861 census, including Edward Gray, a twenty-four-year-old shoemaker. He owned land fronting on the Ninth Line, just north of the lake.

An 1878 Whitchurch Township map shows a brickyard on the Thomas Bolster property, south of Musselman's Lake beside Windsor Lake and just west of the Ninth Line.

Religious needs of local residents were served chiefly by Churchill Christian Church in nearby Churchill. Built in 1872, the church is still holding services. Early lake residents Jacob Musselman (1838–1924), his wife, Emmeline (1849–1940), and son Norman (1885–1905) are buried in the church graveyard.

Gertrude Nighswander, Lake beach, 1902.
Whitchurch-Stouffville Museum

Residents were also served by seasonal churches. St. William's Roman Catholic Church opened its doors only in the summer starting in 1933. Located at Concession Road Nine on Valley Road, the church had Father Martin Johnson as its first priest. Mass was celebrated at the lake in 1926 before the church was built. The church was eventually sold and is now a home. It overlooks Windsor Lake (also known as Mud Lake, for its usually marshy quality).

A small church, called St. Peter's, was apparently erected on Appleton Grove in the early days. The Appleton property, on lot 17, concession 8, was also used as a picnic ground and for various recreational activities.

The community had a summer post office from 1933 to 1969 in a general store called Shalimar. Once opposite a ratepayers' beach at Churchill Drive on the Ninth Line, the store burned down in the late 1970s or early 1980s.

In the early part of the twentieth century, a great change occurred in the area around the lake when it began to be used for recreation. Early development—starting at the time of the first residential plan of subdivision filed in 1919—consisted mainly of cottages, but public park and beach areas were established around the lake: Cedar Beach Park was on the north side, and Cedar Glen, later called Glendale Beach, on the south.

Glendale originally consisted of a hotel and dance hall. The Glen Baker Hotel was built in the late nineteenth century and was destroyed by fire in 1928. The original dance hall was torn down and replaced by one of the largest in the country. This hall was torn down in 1990 after the beach ceased to be used by the public.

Cedar Beach Park went into operation in 1929 when George Davies, Sr., a carpenter, bought the property and constructed a pavilion. In the 1960s his son, Vern, added a trailer park to the operation, which is still a popular summer resort.

The lake now has another trailer facility, Pine Plaza, and a number of general stores. A slaughterhouse once operated at the lake on the property that is now the site of a horseback-riding business. A bowling alley operated for approximately a decade following the Second World War, on the east side of the Ninth Line at the bend in the road.

To the east is 18-acre Shadow Lake, a smaller kettle lake, first known as McKewon Lake for the original landowner, Robert McKewon, who hailed from Ireland. In 1926 it was bought by the T. Eaton Company and used as a summer resort for female employees of the department store. The lake and its surrounding land was sold by Eaton's in 1956, and after the property had changed ownership twice it was purchased in 1966 by the present owners, the Metropolitan Toronto Association for the Mentally Retarded. A 300-acre camp that the association established to serve the developmentally handicapped still exists.

Musselman's Lake gained some notoriety in the 1950s when the bank-robbing Boyd gang came to the community. Gang members Lennie Jackson and Ann Roberts moved into a cottage in 1951 and used it as a hideout and a base for robbing banks in nearby places such as Woodbridge and Bradford.

With the demand for affordable housing in recent decades, Musselman's Lake has changed from a summer resort to a year-round community. In 1956 the lake's population was 358, and in 1966, 201. Cottages were converted to full-time residences. In the 1990s, the lake is now threatened by pollution so ratepayers and politicians are working for a long-term solution to the problem.

CHURCHILL

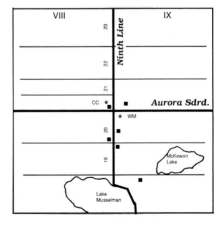

Churchill
Lynne Rubbens

A church on a hill and a family named Hill gave the farming community of Churchill its name.

Located on the crossroads of the Ninth Line (the ninth concession road) and the Aurora Sideroad, the tiny community was settled in the late nineteenth century by farmers, including William Hill, who brought his family to Whitchurch from Ireland in 1812 and settled on land at the southeast corner of the crossroads. The property was in the Hill family until 1920. William Hill not only farmed his land, but he also kept a general store in his home for some of the early years and acted as a lay minister at area churches.

A Methodist church on the Hill farm was the first church in the area. According to a genealogy of the Hill family, churchgoers originally met in the first log schoolhouse built in 1848 on the lake road, but larger quarters were eventually needed. In 1864 a Methodist church was built on the southeast corner of land provided by William Hill. Much of the congregation was lost to the newer Christian church built in the area, so the building fell into disuse and was taken down in 1900.

The community was subsequently held together by its mainstay, Churchill Christian Church, built in 1872 on part of lot 21, concession 8. It began as a Christian church to serve followers who found travelling difficult to the nearest church of the same faith at Bloomington.

George Quantz lived on the 50 acres where the Churchill church still stands on the

northwest side of the Ninth Line, just past the corner of the sideroad. He donated the 1-acre of land where the church was built. Will Badgerow, a Churchill resident, donated the lumber. The flooring was drawn by oxen from Flint's factory in Stouffville. The cemetery was created beside the church in 1929. The graveyard contains the only metal grave-marker seen in this area.

The little church closed for twelve years, except for an occasional service, until the late 1950s. It reopened officially in 1962 as a Baptist church. Additions were made in the 1970s.

Michael Fretz, granted land at lot 21, concession 9, in the mid-1800s, was another of the original settlers. In the 1861 census, he was listed as a thirty-one-year-old farmer born in Canada West (Ontario).

Other early Churchill-area families included the Nesbitts, McMullens, Cleavers, Grays, Reids, Ramers, Streights, Tooles, Pattersons, Lazenbys, Watsons, Widdifields, and later the Forfars and the Paisleys.

The community had no store, post office, blacksmith's shop or school, but relied on neighbouring communities for its necessities. A snack bar opened on the northwest corner of the crossroads in the late 1940s, but it eventually became a towing business and then home of the Whitchurch-Stouffville fire department's second district.

ANOTHER EVEN SMALLER COMMUNITY than Churchill was nearby Palestine, located to the north, at the intersection of the St. John's Sideroad and the Ninth Line. The community was given space for local events in the 1889 *Stouffville Tribune*. The area was later known as Clark's Corners, after property owners. Local children attended school at Vivian (S.S. #5) and residents picked up their mail at Bloomington's post office.

Horse farms and estate homes now stand in the former communities of Churchill and Palestine. Road signs are all that remain of Churchill, while Palestine is just a memory.

*LEFT: **Churchill Church, 1930s.*** Lillian Over and Marjory Holden
*RIGHT: **Albert Clarke farm, St. John's Sideroad, Palestine.***
Marjory Holden

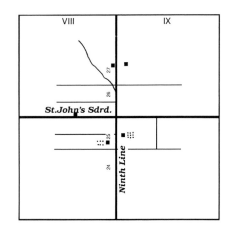

Palestine (Clark's Corners)
Lynne Rubbens

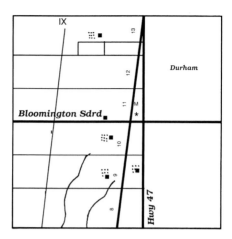

ABOVE: *Lincolnville.* Lynne Rubbens
BELOW: *George Wagg farm, near Lincolnville, 1818.*
Whitchurch-Stouffville Museum

LINCOLNVILLE

The little hamlet of Lincolnville is at the corner of the Bloomington Road and Highway 47 (also known as the old tenth concession road). The community was divided between the townships of Uxbridge on the east and Whitchurch on the west side of the tenth concession road. Tall pines once abounded. They were felled and transported by horse and wagon down the tenth concession road (also known as the mast road) to Lake Ontario for shipment to England, where they were used as masts for sailing vessels.

According to the 1878 *Illustrated Historical Atlas of the County of York*, a Methodist church was located on the west side of the Tenth Line opposite the building that was once the Hammill Hotel. James Hammill, the proprietor, was also the innkeeper at the Garibaldi Hotel in Uxbridge Township. His Lincolnville hotel remains as part of an existing house. Robert Sangster's property was at lot 8, concession 1, of Uxbridge Township. Sangster farmed and operated a basket factory. Also on the Uxbridge side (east side of the tenth concession road) was a Mr. Lehman and William and George Sangster. Water-powered sawmills were located on two of these properties.

Since Lincolnville never grew large enough to support its own school, children in the area attended classes at the Bloomington school (S.S.#10) or the Uxbridge school in Garibaldi.

A short distance north on what is now Regional Road 30 was a steep grade called Gravel Hill, which was first impossible and later merely difficult to negotiate. Large gravel pits were opened many years ago on both sides of the road. The gravel pits remain a successful venture and send a daily procession of trucks along local roads.

Times have changed since the days when farm animals grazed on the roadside and sheep were driven to the local ponds to be washed before being sheared. Only the gravel pits and the remnants of the Hammill Hotel remain to mark the original hamlet of Lincolnville, while modern homes being constructed on Regional Road 30 north of the Bloomington Road are bringing new life to this community. Future plans also include a large industrial park on the Uxbridge side.

ISLAND LAKE

Named for a 1-acre island in the centre of its waters, Island Lake is located at Durham Road 30 and the Aurora Sideroad, split between two municipalities, Whitchurch-Stouffville and Uxbridge, and two regions, York and Durham (then known as York and Ontario counties).

The lake is one of many kettle lakes in the area, formed during the ice age through glacial movement. Another is nearby South Lake.

Farmers who first settled the area in the early nineteenth century were attracted to the excellent land surrounding the 14-acre lake and the fine timber. The lake was already dubbed Island Lake at the time of the 1861 census. Maple, pine, ash, and oak trees surrounded the lake, and the settlers used the wood for their fires. Huge pine trees in the area were used to make 100-foot masts for ships. The lake was also useful, as were other lakes in the area, for its ice in the winter. Ice would be cut by farmers for refrigeration.

Some of the names of landowners appearing in early maps of the area are March, Reid, Yakely, Wagg, Hewlitt, Kellington, Graham, Paisley, and Johnson.

Michael Johnson was originally granted the land that contains the lake, on the southwest corner of the Aurora Sideroad and Durham Road 30. The Crown grant consisted of 77 acres of the east half of lot 20, concession 9. According to a map of Crown grants, Johnson owned the land between 1802 and 1857. A map that shows Whitchurch in 1878 indicates that Frederick Johnson was then owner of the property. By 1904 land registry records state that the property was owned by Thomas Paisley, having been sold by Frederick and Eliza Johnson. According to the 1861 census, a steam sawmill operated by Frederick Johnson was located on the northwest corner of Island Lake on the Johnson property.

Island Lake
Lynne Rubbens

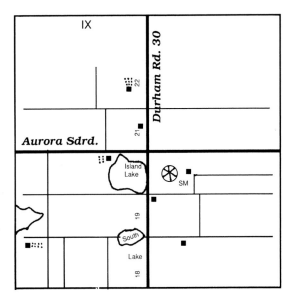

Like many other tiny communities, Island Lake never had its own post office, general store, or school. Instead, the community had to rely on surrounding villages for its needs.

Children on the Whitchurch side went to Ballantrae Public School, west on Aurora Road, while those on the Uxbridge side went to Garibaldi school on the second concession road, even though Ballantrae was much closer.

Recreation became important as the lake area became more settled. By the 1900s the lake was an attractive weekend retreat for both locals and tourists, for swimming and fishing in the summer and skating in the winter.

A tiny cottage, built by Jack Epworth, formerly existed on the tiny island in the middle of the lake, but the island has now been reclaimed by nature. Other cottages were built around the lake.

A little park and beach area were on the corner of the Aurora Sideroad and Durham Road 30 in the mid-1900s. The enterprise even had a food booth. A trailer park stood on the Uxbridge side of the lake, lasting about twenty-five years until industry came to the area when a company manufacturing cigarette lighters opened in 1985.

The area was essentially farming country until after the Second World War. The lake is no longer open to the public and is now surrounded by private estate homes, which a developer started building in 1985.

ABOVE: Island Lake's tiny island.
BELOW: Swimmers at Island Lake, 1930s.
Allan McGillivray

110

CHAPTER 5

THE FUTURE

The Town of Whitchurch-Stouffville is poised on the threshold of major expansion in 1993. The possibility of greater sewage capacity throws Whitchurch-Stouffville open to the large-scale development that has been occurring in surrounding towns for the past ten years. Some taxpayers and politicians welcome expansion for the added jobs, homes, businesses, and tax dollars that could benefit the community. Conversely, residents looking back to an earlier Whitchurch are reluctant to trade their nostalgic images of farms, crossroad villages, and woodlots for subdivisions, shopping malls, and industry.

As buildings age, the cost of repair and renovation lends justification to their removal. Barns no longer housing animals or farm crops are left to disintegrate where they stand. Roads are widened and intersections improved, forcing the demolition of structures that once gave a community its identity. In our increasingly mobile society, few children remain on the family property where they were born. Farms that supported generations of the same family have been sold to developers and sit unused or rented, awaiting development. Many have become golf courses.

Just as Whitchurch-Stouffville looks forward to a prosperous and more highly industrialized future, residents still recognize the values of those born and raised on the land. Parents continue to choose small towns to raise their children because of the safety, the community spirit, and the legacy of the founders.

Quakers, Mennonites, Methodists, Germans, Americans, and Britons all came to Whitchurch in search of a better future for their families. Were they so different from those from diverse cultural and ethnic backgrounds, who are choosing to bring their families to Whitchurch-Stouffville nearly two hundred years later? Surely it is the heritage of those early settlers who arrived in Whitchurch to find a forested wilderness and remained to create communities and farms that has created the substance and spirit of Whitchurch-Stouffville as it exists today.

CHAPTER 6

PHYSICAL GEOGRAPHY

PALAEOZOIC GEOLOGY

The upper to middle Whitby (Collingwood) Formation bedrock on which most of Whitchurch Township is situated resulted when sediments were laid down on ancient ocean floors during the Ordovician Period about 450 million years ago. Two areas, (i) north of the Whitchurch-Markham town line between Wilcox Lake and Haynes Lake, comprising about 800 to 1000 acres, and (ii) a triangular slice of land between Aurora and Newmarket in the first concession of Whitchurch entailing a further 2000 acres, are underlain by bedrock belonging to the Georgian Bay (Dundas) Formation. Geologically, the Georgian Bay Formation bedrock was laid down about five to ten million years after the sediments that make up the Whitby Formation.

Whitby Formation bedrock is composed of dark brownish grey to black, thinly bedded fissile shale. The formation is about 200 feet thick. Although there are no known exposures of this bedrock in Whitchurch, there is an outcrop of Whitby shale in the third concession of Pickering Township. The bedding of shale thickens near the bottom of the exposed section, and it is covered with an overburden 20 to 30 feet thick. Chemical analysis of Whitby shale suggests that it might be suitable for a lightweight aggregate. The Georgian Bay (Dundas) Formation shales, which again do not outcrop in the township, are greenish grey to medium grey in colour and are sometimes interbedded with grey limestone and grey siltstone. This interbedding decreases towards the base of the formation, which is in places up to 300 feet thick. Georgian Bay (Dundas) shale is exposed at the Don Valley Brick Yard, where it is quarried for use in the manufacture of brick.

PLEISTOCENE GEOLOGY

DURING THE PERIOD known as the Pleistocene, which spans the past 1.5 million years, there have been at least four major episodes of glacial ice movement that have impacted on northeastern North America. The Quaternary sediments that overlie Whitchurch Township were deposited as the result of ice movements associated with the northeastward retreat of glacial ice during the last of these four glacial stages, known as the late Wisconsinan (about twenty-five thousand to ten thousand years ago).

The Wisconsin glacier reached its maximum southern limits along the Shelbyville-Olive moraine systems in southern Ohio and central Pennsylvania about 21,500 years ago. With minor fluctuations the ice sheet remained near this limit until about seventeen thousand years ago when milder climatic conditions began to cause melting and the subsequent recession of the glacial ice lobes to the north-northeast. The latter stages associated with the wasting of the Wisconsin glacier entailed a complex series of events whereby the ice retreated, advanced, and retreated again on a number of occasions along regionalized fronts. In periods of climatic warming, known as interstades, the ice retreated and large meltwater lakes formed in front of the ice margins. During colder periods, known as stades, the ice readvanced and overrode previously deglaciated areas. In the process of advancing, the thickening ice pushed over forests and totally reshaped the landscape. Plant and animal communities in the path of ice advances of this nature were of necessity forced to migrate to areas below the new ice boundaries.

HOLOCENE PHYSIOGRAPHY

THE PRINCIPAL PHYSIOGRAPHIC FEATURES that make up the landscape of Whitchurch Township were formed during the final stages of ice retreat during the Late Pleistocene. During the past ten thousand years, known as the Holocene, these features have undergone slow but continual changes that help form the physical region we know today. The three major physiographic features of the township include: (i) the Oak Ridges kame moraine, (ii) the Schomberg Lake plain, and (iii) the drumlinized till plains, of which the Markham-Pickering till plain is the predominant subregion.

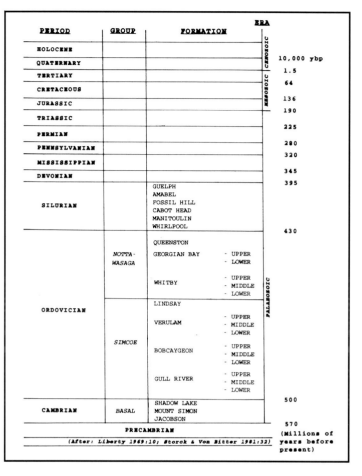

Bedrock formations of south-central Ontario.
York North Archaeological Services

Oak Ridges Kame Moraine

THE OAK RIDGES KAME MORAINE cuts across the township from west to east along a band about 3 to 4 miles in width. There is a lobate section, a rounded projection, of this feature along the eastern side of the township that extends northward into East Gwillimbury. In Whitchurch, the moraine takes the form of a highland area consisting of knobby sand hills with elevations ranging from about 950 to 1,225 feet above sea level.

The term "kame," a hill or ridge deposited by retreating glaciers, used to describe the Oak Ridges kame moraine, is based on the high percentage of kames in the interlobate section of the moraine. They were formed when glacial meltwater poured off the ice sheet, carrying deposits of sand and gravel that built up along the ice margins. Kames are generally composed of irregularly bedded and crossbedded deposits of sand and gravel that take the form of hills

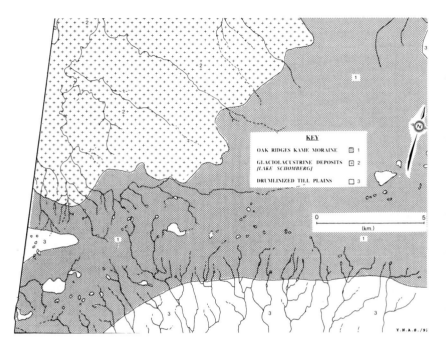

or knobs. The sands and kame deposits associated with the Oak Ridges kame moraine are extensively mined in eastern Whitchurch and adjacent sections of Uxbridge Township.

There is a possible glacial spillway associated with the southeastern section of the moraine in lots 8 and 9, concessions 4 to 8 of Whitchurch. According to Ontario Department of Mines geologist D.F. Hewitt, once the Lake Ontario lobe retreated to the area of the Whitchurch-Markham town line, gravel accumulated along the southern margins of Whitchurch Township. When the Ontario ice readvanced it briefly covered the southern slope of the Oak Ridges kame moraine, capping it with a clay till. The gravel deposits in lots 8 and 9, concessions 4 to 8, appear to mark the course of an east-west glacial spillway that flowed westerly along the ice front when the lobe was halted at that position.

Physiographic areas of Whitchurch Township
York North Archaeological Services

Schomberg Lake Plain

THE SCHOMBERG LAKE PLAIN makes up most of the northwest corner of Whitchurch Township, from the edges of the towns of Newmarket and Aurora as far east as Cedar Valley. Underlying the western part of the former lake bed are silty varved clays and some minor till deposits. The eastern part of the area, along the margins of the Oak Ridges kame moraine, is overlain by silts and fine sands. The lake plain ranges in elevation from 850 to 950 feet above sea level, and the eastern part of the area is somewhat irregular in topography.

Drumlinized Till Plains

THE LARGEST TILL PLAIN in Whitchurch is located between concessions 3 and 10, below the southern margins of the Oak Ridges kame moraine. The clay loam till that makes up this plain is, in places, capped with a thin veneer of clay, silt, or fine sands that were deposited during the period of the Peel-Schomberg pondings. Situated along the till plains in Whitchurch are a number of features known as drumlins. These hills are oval in shape and are often a quarter of a mile to a mile in length but seldom exceed a quarter of a mile in width. They often stand 50 to 75 feet above the till plain. Drumlins consist mostly of medium-textured boulder clay, and while there is a considerable portion of sand and clay in the constituent tills, the extremes of heavy clay or light sands are seldom found.

In addition to the above large drumlinized till plain in southern Whitchurch, there are small sections of till plain in three other areas of the township: (i) along Yonge Street to the northwest of Wilcox Lake, (ii) in the extreme northwest corner of the former Township of

Whitchurch, now within the Town of Newmarket and (iii) in the northeast corner of the township to the immediate east of Vivian Creek.

DRAINAGE

THE TOP OF THE OAK RIDGES KAME MORAINE is a watershed from which local drainage flows in two directions. The East Holland River, Black River, and Vivian Creek flow northward into the Lake Simcoe basin, while the headwaters streams for the East Humber River, Rouge River, Bruce Creek and Duffins Creek flow southward into the Lake Ontario basin. Dotted along the top of the moraine in Whitchurch are numerous kettle lakes or ponds. Some of the better known include, from west to east, Bond, Wilcox, St. George, Preston, Van Nostrand, Clark, and Musselman's lakes. These lakes, which are often quite deep, are the results of blocks of ice that, left behind by the retreating glacier, were buried in such a way that when they melted, depressions were formed, subsequently becoming filled with water.

SOILS

SOILS ARE GENERALLY FORMED from the underlying parent material upon which they reside. Often the parent material is bedrock, but in Whitchurch, as in other areas where glacial action has deposited unconsolidated materials from afar, the parent material is that which was left behind most recently by the retreating Lake Simcoe–Georgian Bay and Ontario ice lobes.

Soils formed over the former bed of glacial Lake Schomberg in the northwest corner of the township belong to the Schomberg clay and loam series. These former lake-bottom soils are generally grey calcareous clays and silty clays. The land is moderately smooth to irregular steeply sloping and often well drained. Large portions of this area have been used for agriculture in the past, but with the expansion of communities such as Newmarket and Aurora, once arable farmland is currently being developed at a previously unprecedented rate.

Below the Oak Ridges kame moraine along the south-central and southeastern end of the township, the soils mostly belong to the Woburn and Milliken loam series. Both of these loams are formed over medium-textured, brown shaly calcareous tills. Woburn series soils are often found in topographically steeper localities than Milliken soils, and they are also better drained. At the very southern edge of the township, there are small pockets of Peel clay, which tend to overlay the former Peel Ponds. Peel clay soils are lacustrine in origin and often overlay gritty clays at depths of 3 feet or less. The drainage is often imperfect, and the topography is smooth to very gently sloping.

Soils along the Oak Ridges kame moraine belong mostly to the Pontypool and Woburn sandy and sandy loam series. The Pontypool series consists of poorly sorted calcareous outwash soils, while the Woburn soils have been formed over medium-textured brown shaly calcareous tills. Both soil series are well drained and have smooth to irregularly steep slopes. To the north-northwest of Musselman's Lake, there is also a fairly large pocket of Brighton sandy loam. This series consists of well-sorted grey calcareous sands or stratified sands and gravels. These soils are well drained, and the topography is smooth to very gently sloping. Along the moraine to

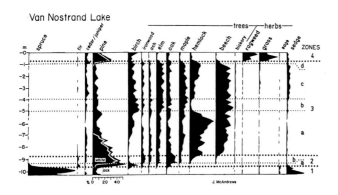

Van Nostrand Lake

Pollen diagram of Van Nostrand Lake.
York North Archaeological Services

the northeast of Vandorf, considerable areas had to be reforested during the early part of this century owing to the light and unstable nature of the sandy topsoil.

Areas with muck soils are found mostly along the headwaters streams of the East Holland and Black rivers. There are two other notable muck-soil areas in the township, near Preston Lake and to the northwest of Lake St. George. Muck soils are formed over well-decomposed organic deposits and are very poorly drained. Soils of this nature are often suitable for market-garden farming.

VEGETATION COMMUNITIES
(Holocene Reconstruction)

THE POLLEN DIAGRAM for Van Nostrand Lake provides an outline of the vegetation changes that have taken place along the southern margins of the white pine hardwood forest region of southern Ontario since the recession of the ice. From a 33-foot sediment core extracted from the bottom of Van Nostrand Lake, four broadly defined pollen zones have been recognized. Zone 1 entails the lower 1½-foot of sediment and represents material broadly defined as glacial drift. The vegetation from this zone is dominated by spruce and sedge pollen and is analogous to the vegetation present in the forest-tundra zone of northern Canada today. This zone dates from deglaciation to about ten thousand years ago.

Zone 2, also known as the pine zone, is divided into two subzones. Subzone 2a is dominated by jack pine comparable to that in the northern boreal forest, and Subzone 2b is dominated by white pine similar to that in the southern boreal forest. The sediments in this zone consist of organic silts that were likely derived form sparsely vegetated soils along the uplands adjacent to the lake margin. At Van Nostrand Lake a Carbon 14 date of 9,750 years ago marks the transition between Subzones 2a and 2b.

In Zone 3, the vegetation is dominated by hemlock, elm, pine, beech, maple, and other members of the mixed forest community. There are four recognized subzones in Pollen Zone 3. Subzone 3a has abundant hemlock that drops to a minimum in 3b, with the boundary being Carbon 14 dated at 5,710 years ago. At Van Nostrand Lake this pine rise is attributable to regrowth in abandoned corn fields associated with a protohistoric Iroquoian settlement located less than 3 miles from the coring site. Most of the sediment in this zone is a lime-rich organic mud known as marl which was formed by algae in the lake.

In Pollen Zone 4 there is abundant ragweed and grass pollen that represent changes to the adjacent landscape as a result of modern European agriculture during the past century. The upper 3 feet of the above sediment core is mostly clay that has been derived from the erosion of the adjacent upland soils following nineteenth-century forest clearance.

CHAPTER 7

ARCHAEOLOGY

As the pioneer farming community began to open tracts of Whitchurch Township from its unbroken forest canopy in the early nineteenth century, workers found among the stumps and along the newly turned furrows projectile points, stone adzes, carbonized plant and animal remains, and, of course, some evidence of human burials. As in other parts of the North American continent, the discovery of archaeological remains generally resulted in the creation of fanciful theories to explain events associated with the distant past. The earliest archaeological discoveries were often interpreted as either the remnants of some lost pre-contact civilization or as an ancient battleground where skirmishes between native groups and the earliest Euro-American settlers once took place. In fact, most of the artifacts represented long-abandoned campsites or villages and the hunting- and farming-related implements used by former inhabitants in their day-to-day quest for economic survival.

PALAEO-INDIAN PERIOD (9000–7500 B.C.)
THE FIRST PALAEO-INDIAN HUNTING BANDS likely entered southwestern Ontario from the Ohio-Michigan area sometime around 9000 B.C. As most of the known Palaeo-Indian sites in southern Ontario have been found along the shorelines of glacial lakes, it is hypothesized that multi-family hunting groups gathered on a seasonal basis at strategic game-migration routes in order to intercept herd animals such as caribou. Hare, ptarmigan, and other small barrenland fringe species would also have been hunted. A number of Palaeo-Indian base camps have been found by archaeologists along glacial shorelines in southern Ontario, at sites such as Fisher, Parkhill, Udora, and Deavitt, where large communal hunts likely took place. These places are almost always strategically located in relation to topographic barriers that could impede the rapid movement of game such as caribou, during the annual migration from their spring calving grounds along the barren grounds to their more southerly boreal forest edge wintering ranges. The possibility exists that larger mammals such as mammoth and mastodon were also hunted when the occasion presented itself, along the edge of the boreal forest.

As Whitchurch is a considerable distance inland from the shorelines of either glacial Lake Algonquin or Iroquois, the presence of at least two small Palaeo-Indian components in the

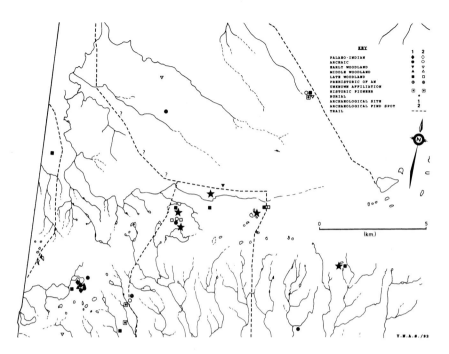

KEY

PALAEO-INDIAN
ARCHAIC
EARLY WOODLAND
MIDDLE WOODLAND
LATE WOODLAND
PREHISTORIC OF AN
UNKNOWN AFFILIATION
HISTORIC PIONEER
BURIAL
ARCHAEOLOGICAL SITE
ARCHAEOLOGICAL FIND SPOT
TRAIL

*Archaeological sites and find spots
recorded in Whitchurch Township.*
York North Archaeological Services

vicinity of Lake St. George suggests that these sites were used by family-sized groups hunting small wintering maternity herds of caribou. The Esox sites in the George Lake Conservation Area are in close proximity to late-glacial ice block–kettle lake depressions. In the study of prehistoric habitats, archaeologists are only beginning to examine the importance of these localized kettle-swamp-stream environments and their role throughout prehistory in attracting settlement. In addition to being favoured by Palaeo-Indians, the Lake St. George and Esox sites were subsequently occupied during the Archaic, Early, and Middle Woodland periods.

To the south of the Whitchurch town line, in Vaughan Township, the remains of a mammoth were uncovered in the 1830s, during the excavation of a mill race. Although there is no evidence to suggest that this animal was killed by human agents, the presence of mammoth in the immediate area suggests another local resource that could have been exploited by Palaeo-Indian hunters.

ARCHAIC PERIOD (7500–1000 B.C.)

THE ARCHAIC EVOLVED from the previous Palaeo-Indian cultural base in response to changing environmental conditions. As climatic zones shifted farther north, certain of the Late Palaeo-Indian groups of necessity migrated northward and continued their traditional tundra-boreal forest edge life-styles as caribou hunters, while other groups took up residence in regions being colonized by the deciduous forest. Whereas certain of the technologies and life-styles were derived from the earlier cultural base, newer ideas and technologies were imported into the region from Archaic groups living to the south of the Great Lakes. As part of their annual subsistence cycle, Archaic groups operated at the microband (extended-family) level during the fall and winter, collecting nuts and hunting small animals attracted to the deciduous forest. During the spring and summer, when resources were more abundant, macroband (a number of microband or family-group) settlements would have been created at places where large quantities of aquatic resources could be harvested. During these macroband gatherings exotic artifacts and new ideas would have been exchanged and external family bonds made.

A small number of Archaic components have been found in Whitchurch, but for the most part they consist of isolated artifacts, such as projectile points, which were often lost during the course of hunting activities. The most promising evidence for an Archaic campsite within the township was unfortunately destroyed during the expansion of the Spring Lakes Golf Course at Ringwood in 1981. Artifacts recovered from the Spring Lakes property include a number of late Archaic broadpoints, two knives, and a ground stone celt. The chipped-stone artifacts are all manufactured from Onondaga chert, which was brought into the area from quarries along the north shore of Lake Erie. This former encampment probably dates from about 1500 B.C. Archaic artifacts have also been found at the Preston, Lake St. George, and Goforth sites. A projectile point from the Goforth site has a bificate base and probably dates from the early Archaic period.

Archaic artifacts from Spring Lakes Golf Club site.
York North Archaeological Services

WOODLAND PERIOD (1000 B.C.–1650 A.D.)

THE WOODLAND PERIOD comprises three sub-periods: Early (1000 B.C.–0 A.D.), Middle (0 A.D.–1000 A.D.) and Late Woodland (1000 A.D.–1650 A.D.). The Late Woodland period sites in Whitchurch can in turn be divided into three sub-periods: Pickering, Middle Ontario Iroquois, and Late Iroquoian.

Early Woodland (1000 B.C.–0 A.D.)

THIS PERIOD IS DIVIDED into two sub-periods: Meadowood (c. 1000 B.C.–400 B.C.) and Middlesex (400 B.C.–0 A.D.). Economic pursuits during the Early Woodland were similar to the Archaic in that hunting, fishing, and gathering were still the primary subsistence activities. It was during the Early Woodland that ceramics were first introduced into southern Ontario. There is evidence from the archaeological record that mortuary practices became more elaborate during this period.

In Whitchurch there are a number of archaeological sites where Early Woodland artifacts have been found. Two Meadowood projectile points were found at the Goforth site in the seventh concession, and two Middlesex period projectile points are included in a private collection of artifacts found at the Devins tree farm. The Lake St. George site on Metropolitan Toronto and Region Conservation Authority lands also includes an Early Woodland component. Two isolated finds, of either ceremonial or high-status artifacts, which probably date from the Early Woodland period, have also been recorded within the township. A circular ground slate gorget was found near Vandorf, and a birdstone (probably a weight) was found to the southeast of Newmarket along the Bogart creek.

Middle Woodland (0 A.D.–800 A.D.)

DURING THE MIDDLE WOODLAND PERIOD, settlement-subsistence activities remained much the same as they had been during the Early Woodland. Some of the notable changes during this period include a more pronounced exploitation of fish during their spring spawning, and towards the end of the Middle Woodland, corn was introduced into southern Ontario. Social changes, especially in regard to mortuary practices, were influenced by contact with peoples living south of the Great Lakes. The most pronounced evidence of an Early Woodland burial complex in southern Ontario is the Serpent Mounds along the north shore of Rice Lake.

In the extreme southwest corner of the township, three Middle Woodland components have been identified at the Lake St. George, Esox, and Rodes sites.

Late Woodland (800 A.D.–1650 A.D.)

THE LATE WOODLAND PERIOD ushered in major changes in the settlement-subsistence practices associated with southern Ontario's native peoples. Complex changes were brought about largely as the result of an increased reliance on agriculture. As the social complexity increased, populations became politically aligned into regionally distinct tribal groups. Associated with this period are settlements of various sizes, ranging from small encampments to hamlets and large villages. Late Woodland archaeological sites were often built upon strategically located hilltops and protected by palisades. Burial practices varied from individual interments to community cemeteries and communal burial pits, known as ossuaries.

Pickering (800 A.D.–1300 A.D.)

PICKERING SUBSISTENCE PRACTICES included both corn agriculture and hunting and fishing. Archaeological sites associated with the Pickering culture were primarily located in south-central Ontario, while at the same time a somewhat similar group known as Glen Meyer occupied sites in southwestern Ontario. About 1300 A.D. a portion of the Pickering population migrated into southwestern Ontario and conquered the Glen Meyer (both were Iroquois). Although the Glen Meyer probably ceased to exist at this point as an independent people it is likely that large portions of their numbers would have been amalgamated into the Pickering groups.

As a result of a number of sites having been either excavated or extensively tested in south-central Ontario, it is possible to make statements concerning Pickering traits beyond the level of recoverable material artifacts. Along Duffins Creek, to the northwest of Ajax, the Miller site was almost completely excavated in 1958. This village dating to about 1125 A.D. was palisaded and contained a number of large rectangular houses. One of the houses was 57 feet in length by 24 feet in width and possessed a line of five central hearths. A number of multiple secondary-type burials were found in and around the village, but they contained little or no grave goods. Large quantities of both dentate (toothed) and linear stamped motif ceramics were recovered from the Miller excavations. At the Upper Nursery site in the Boyd Conservation Area in Vaughan Township a small Pickering encampment was partially excavated in 1981. The proximity of this site to the Humber River suggests it may have been so situated in order to exploit seasonal aquatic resources. A radiocarbon date of 900 A.D. was obtained

120

from a hearth feature associated with this site, but neither contemporaneous faunal (animal) remains or ceramics were recovered.

In Whitchurch two Pickering components have been located at the Wilcox Lake and Goforth sites. At Wilcox Lake, salvage excavations in 1988 unearthed a section of a curved house wall and a cluster of interior pit features. The ceramic assemblage includes a nearly complete vessel dominated by a collarless rim form and paddle-marked body decoration. A single linear stamped rim sherd from the Goforth site suggests a possible occupation about the same time as the late Pickering Miller site, about 850 to eight hundred years ago.

MIDDLE ONTARIO IROQUOIS (1300 A.D.–1400 A.D.)

IT WAS DURING the Middle Ontario Iroquois (aka Middleport) period that the Pickering expansion westward occurred and a common cultural base population was formed. Middle Ontario Iroquoian groups lived in palisaded semi-permanent villages and practised corn agriculture. The villages were sometimes as much as 3 to 5 acres in size. Burial practices included interment in ossuaries. Grave goods were seldom buried with the dead.

The only known Middle Ontario Iroquois component in Whitchurch is associated with the Goforth site. A single rim sherd from this component has four rows of horizontal linear trailing below a very narrow dentate stamped collar. Tentatively this sherd is identified as a variant of a Middle Ontario Iroquois Ontario Horizontal motif.

LATE ONTARIO IROQUOIS (1400 A.D.–1650 A.D.)

ABOUT 1400 A.D. Middle Ontario Iroquois base populations branched into the four major Iroquoian groups present in south-central and southwestern Ontario at the time of arrival of the first Europeans. Middle Ontario Iroquois populations living along the rivers and streams to the north of Lake Ontario developed along community lines into the Huron and Petun groups who were found residing in Huronia and Petunia (between Creemore and Collingwood) at the time of the visit of the French explorer Champlain in 1615, while Middle Ontario Iroquoian populations living in southwestern Ontario amalgamated to form the Neutral and Erie groups. To a degree most of the Late Iroquoian period showed relatively stable settlement and subsistence patterns. The exceptions to this, of course, being the dispersal of the St. Lawrence Iroquois and amalgamation of elements of their population with Huron groups during the early Proto-Historic period, and the post-1640s era when intertribal warfare was brought to the heart of both Huronia and Neutralia by the Five Nations Iroquois from upstate New York.

Villages during the Late Iroquoian period were palisaded and often situated slightly off navigable waterways, upon hilltops chosen for defensive reasons. Houses sometimes exceeded 262 or more feet in length, and they had storage vestibules located at the two ends. Along the centre of the dwellings was a row of central hearths that were tended by family-based living units. As a result of soil exhaustion and the depletion of nearby woodlots for consumable firewood, villages were forced to relocate every ten to twenty years. Within the community

context, females tended the fields and harvested the annual crops of corn, beans and squash. Male members of the community tended to construction-related activities associated with village relocation, hunting, and village defence.

Burial practices included a number of different types of interment: individual, cemetery, and communal ossuary. During the historic period, considerable quantities of material possessions were occasionally interred with the deceased individual or individuals.

To date a total of six Late Iroquoian sites have been recorded within the boundaries of Whitchurch, as follows:

Northern Railway Depot Site

THIS SITE was at the Northern Railway Depot in Aurora and was likely destroyed during the course of railway construction in the 1850s. Artifact collections are not known to exist for this site.

Ruben Heise Site

THE RUBEN HEISE SITE is along one of the Rouge River headwater streams in the southwest corner of Whitchurch. Artifacts collected from the site suggest that it was occupied between 1500 and 1550 A.D. A lack of historic trade material suggests that the site may date from nearer the early part of this period.

Ratcliff Site

THIS SITE IS ALONG ONE of the upper headwater tributaries of the Rouge River along the southern flanks of the Oak Ridges moraine. A ravine along the west edge of the site was in-filled during the early 1950s in order to allow for the expansion of a nearby quarry.

On the basis of archaeological investigations at the Ratcliff site, a number of observations can be made concerning the Iroquoian populations who once lived here. The ceramics indicate strong similarities to Southern Division Huron groups. However, there are less frequent examples of the ceramic types known as Roebuck Corn Ear, Dutch Hollow Notched and Warminster Crossed that suggest contacts with groups residing in both upstate New York and the St. Lawrence Valley.

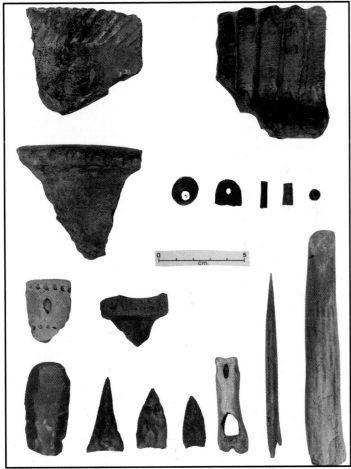

ABOVE: Royal Ontario Museum excavation at the Commercial Sand and Gravel property in 1954. Royal Ontario Museum BELOW: Artifacts from the Ratcliff site. York North Archaeological Services

The large quantity of both ground and chipped stone, in all stages of manufacture from the Ratcliff site, suggests that this village had a special function in the regional production and redistribution of stone artifacts. Most of the chipped-stone artifacts are of Onondaga chert, which would have been transported in bulk into the area from quarries along the Niagara Peninsula. At other Late Iroquoian sites, along the Duffins-Rouge-Humber drainages, which were more or less contemporaneous with Ratcliff, similar quantities of lithic artifacts and accompanying manufacturing debris are seldom found.

European trade items include one black glass bead, copper and brass beads, and miscellaneous copper and brass fragments.

The faunal sample includes chicken, pig, and possibly domestic dog, which have been deposited on the site as a result of waste-disposal operations associated with the adjacent farmstead. Species utilized by the villages include beaver, porcupine, black bear, raccoon, marten, river otter, American elk, white-tailed deer, wild turkey, blue heron, sucker, bass, salmon, and clam.

There was an ossuary reportedly opened to the north of the Ratcliff site in the mid-1850s, and a nearby grouping of four burials was excavated by archaeologists in 1954. Investigations at the site about 1850 also discovered a human skull gorget, which was likely a war trophy.

Information currently available concerning Ratcliff suggests that this site dates from the 1525–1575 period and is possibly one of the sites that formed after the dissolution of the Draper community, which was located 7 miles to the southeast, near Atha Road. The presence of glass beads and a small amount of copper and/or brass indicate that the site is Proto-Historic and was likely in contact with other groups trading with either the French in the St. Lawrence Valley or the Dutch to the south, whose goods were beginning to filter up the Susquehanna and into southern Ontario by the early sixteenth century.

Aurora Site

THIS SITE IS LOCATED along one of the headwater tributaries of the East Holland River on the north side of the Oak Ridges moraine. Along two sides of the site there are steep ravines, and the East Holland River and one of its tributaries form the boundaries of the other two sides.

Over the years this site has been very heavily looted, and a lot of potential information concerning native life has been indiscriminately destroyed in the quest for collections to fill curio shelves. Respected amateur archaeologist Peter Pringle's map shows the boundaries of the site in the 1930s.

On the basis of the analysis of ceramic artifacts, it is suggested that Aurora dates from the early Proto-Historic period. The possibility exists that this site was in part occupied by one of the groups who had previously settled at the McKenzie site in Woodbridge. When the Aurora site was abandoned some of its inhabitants likely moved to the north-northeast and made up part of the base population resident at the Warminster site. The Warminster, or Cahiague site, is at the north end of Lake Simcoe, and it is thought to be the place where Champlain wintered in 1615 during his visit to Huronia. A small number of historic trade

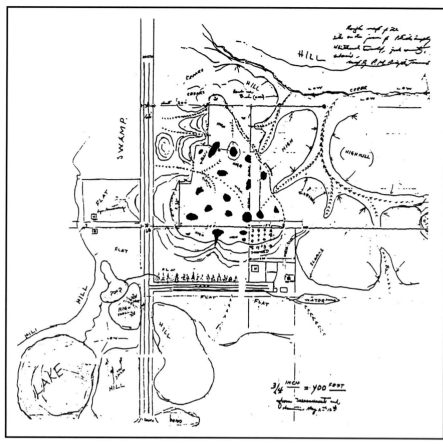

items have been found at the Aurora site, adding credence to the suggestion that the site was occupied about 1525–1575 A.D.

Burials have been found near the Aurora site and to the south west overlooking Clark Lake. All burial descriptions for the immediate area suggest either isolated or cemetery interments.

Hoshel Site

THE HOSHEL SITE IS A SMALL VILLAGE or hamlet about 1¼ miles to the west of the Aurora site. It is bordered by steep slopes along its east and west sides but has no natural defence to the south. As the nearest drainage is about 820 feet to the north, it is possible that potable water was obtained from nearby springs. Most of the data available are based on the analysis of materials excavated from a midden (refuse heap) along the north end of the site.

The ceramics are a mixture of both Huron-Petun and Neutral types. Most of the ceramic types are similar to materials excavated from the Seed-Barker site near Pine Grove in Vaughan Township. It is suggested on the basis of the ceramics that people who resided at the Hoshel site were closely aligned with elements of the Neutral population at the Seed-Barker site. Two iron knife blades and two copper or brass fragments suggest that this is a Proto-Historic site probably occupied from 1550 to 1600.

A burial found during the course of sand quarrying on the south side of the Vandorf Sideroad in 1935 and a number of burials associated with an apparent cemetery farther to the north east, near the East Holland River, may be associated with the Hoshel site.

Vandorf (Van Nostrand-Wright) Site

THE VANDORF SITE IS LOCATED along the Oak Ridges moraine overlooking Van Nostrand Lake. There are steep embankments along its northern and western margins. When the Vandorf site was occupied, potable water could have been obtained from up to three local sources: (i) a headwater stream to the East Holland River along the western side of the site; (ii) from springs associated with a former streambed along the site's eastern margins; or (iii) from Van Nostrand Lake.

Archaeological investigations at the Vandorf site have been confined to a surface survey of two small sections of the former village area. The Vandorf ceramics are again a mixture of Huron-Petun and Neutral types. However, the Neutral ceramic elements are not as prevalent at Vandorf as they were found to be at the slightly earlier Hoshel site.

The small faunal sample has yet to be analyzed to determine individual faunal elements or species. In the private collections from the site, there are a number of faunal specimens that have been modified for use as either decorative or utilitarian artifacts. A number of bird bones were scored and in some instances cut into beads. There is also a bear canine pendant and a bone netting needle within the sample.

At Vandorf, the lithic (stone tool) sample is very small. This is probably a result of the increasing reliance on metal within the community, which would have shifted the emphasis from stone-tool production to the recycling of metal artifacts for everyday use. The four artifact collections available for study from Vandorf include at least fifty European trade items made of either brass/copper, iron, or glass. Categories of trade goods or items manufactured from recycled trade goods include: copper or brass beads, knives, projectile points, iron knives, axes, spuds and a fishhook, and one light blue glass bead.

The quantity of trade items suggests that this site dates from either the very late Proto-Historic or early Historic periods, between 1590 and 1615. The peoples who lived at Vandorf were likely ancestral Huron-Petun who were influenced somewhat by nearby contemporaneous Neutral groups.

The burial ground associated with Vandorf is located within two-thirds of a mile of the edge of the village.

Select artifacts from the Vandorf site.
York North Archaeological Services

ISOLATED LATE WOODLAND FIND SPOTS

TWO ARTIFACTS HAVE BEEN FOUND from isolated contexts in the area to the immediate south of the Vandorf site. These artifacts—an iron knife blade and a large folded section of a copper or brass kettle—are both historic trade items and probably date fromo the same period as the adjacent Iroquois villages at Vandorf or Hoshel.

APPENDIX A

CHURCHES

Providence, Second Markham Springvale Baptist. Whitchurch-Stouffville Museum

Records of the earliest churches of Whitchurch are often difficult to find. We know that many of the early settlers of the township held strong religious beliefs and continued to practise their religion during the early days of settlement, often in one another's homes. Quakers and Mennonites settled entire communities and established meetings as soon as trails could be cleared between lots. Other religious groups also established early places of worship, many of them log churches that have since disappeared. Some buildings erected as places of worship for one congregation have since been converted to other purposes or have been sold to another denomination. Several of the early denominations have changed their names since their formation, while others have united to form new churches.

Only those churches in the towns of Aurora and Newmarket that had been established prior to incorporation have been included in this listing. In the remainder of Whitchurch-Stouffville, only those churches established before the mid-1900s have been included.

The following list of dates is incomplete; numerous congregations met for many years before an actual building was erected. The dates given represent the earliest and latest records available for the church buildings. Further information on many of these churches is available in the Whitchurch-Stouffville Museum archives.

METHODIST CHURCHES

During the 1800s four branches of the Methodist Church were established in Canada. These were the Methodist Episcopal, the Wesleyan Methodists, the New Connexion, and the Primitive Methodists. By 1884 these various branches along with the Bible Christian Churches combined to form the Methodist Church in Canada. In 1925 the Methodist Church joined with the Congregational Church and a part of the Presbyterian Church to form the United Church of Canada.

Location	Earliest Records	Church Still Active	Date of Existing Building	Current Name	Additional Information
Aurora	1818	yes	1878	Aurora United	Two additional Methodist churches existed in Aurora in the early 1800s. Both buildings remain on Mosley Street and are now used for other purposes.
Newmarket	1824	yes	1880	Trinity United	Services prior to 1880 were held in buildings at the northeast corner of Prospect and Timothy Streets.
White Rose		no	demolished 1884		An early log church.

Location	Earliest Records	Church Still Active	Date of Existing Building	Current Name	Additional Information
White Rose	1870	no	demolished 1970		Named Mount Pisgah.
Bethesda	1855	no	1855		Originally built of wood; later bricked; closed 1969; privately owned.
Lemonville	1856	yes	1856	Lemonville United	Used briefly as a Dutch Reform church in 1950s.
Ballantrae	1878	yes	1939	St. Georgio Orthodox	Remained Ballantrae United Church till the 1980s. The 1878 building burnt down in 1939.
Hartman	1863	no	1899		Closed in 1967; privately owned.
Bloomington	1869	no			Building sold and moved in 1939 to Buttonville, where it is in use as a community hall.
Churchill	1864	no	demolished in 1900		Met in log schoolhouse built in 1848 before church building was erected.
Lincolnville		no			No information available.
Hartman's Corners	1878	no			Building moved to Aurora, and used as blacksmith's shop on Yonge Street.
Wesley Corners	1841	yes	1881	Wesley United Church	Original log church known as Petch's Chapel.
Stouffville	1841	yes	1892	Stouffville United Church	First services held in school, then in 1872 brick building.

PRESBYTERIAN CHURCHES

Location	Earliest Records	Church Still Active	Date of Existing Building	Current Name	Additional Information
Newmarket	1845	yes	1875 1992	St. Andrews	Congregation worshipped in building at Garbutt Hill on Prospect Street until 1875. In 1992 a new sanctuary was added.
Ballantrae	1878	no	burned 1970		Original building was moved to Musselman's Lake in 1924; rebuilt after 1970 to serve as a United church.
Stouffville	1860	yes	1894	St. James	First church erected 1863.

CONGREGATIONAL CHURCHES

The Congregationalists originated in England in the early days of Protestantism. Their name came from their central belief that the congregation was answerable directly to God, not via a priest or minister. In 1925 the majority of Congregationalist churches voted to unite with Methodists and Presbyterians to form the United Church of Canada.

Location	Earliest Records	Church Still Active	Date of Existing Building	Current Name	Additional Information
Stouffville	1842	yes	1875	Memorial Christian Church	First building erected in 1847 in the east end. In 1875 a new building was constructed at Stouffer and Main streets. The congregation reorganized as a Christian church in 1903.
Newmarket	1842	no			Church on Botsford Street?

CHRISTIAN CHURCHES

The Christian Church, from the United States, was active in Canada in the 1820s. Sometimes confused with the Congregational Church because adherents followed a congregational form of organization, or with other unrelated churches bearing similar names, the Christian Church established itself in many small communities in southern Ontario at a time when travel to larger centres and their churches was difficult and the local church formed the heart of the community.

Location	Earliest Records	Church Still Active	Date of Existing Building	Current Name	Additional Information
Stouffville	1842	yes	1875	Memorial Christian Church	1842-1902 This church was the Stouffville Congregational Church, reorganized as Memorial Christian Church in 1903.
Ringwood	1824	yes	1868	Ringwood Congregational Christian Church	
Churchill	1872	yes	1872	Churchill Baptist Church	After the building was closed for twelve years, a Baptist congregation acquired it and began services in 1962.
Bloomington	1833	yes	1892	Bloomington Christian Gospel Church	Disassociated from the Christian Conference and became affiliated with the Associated Gospel Churches of Ontario in 1956.
Newmarket	1822	yes	1874	The Christian Baptist Church	Received into the Baptist Convention of Ontario and Quebec in 1949.
Pine Orchard	1873	no	torn down in 1950s		Met in Temperance Hall, Lot 31.

MENNONITE/ MISSIONARY CHURCHES

In the early 1800s, several large groups of Mennonite families from Pennsylvania settled in the Markham and Stouffville areas. The founding Stouffer family of Stouffville was among them. These families often worshipped in their homes or barns for several years before erecting church buildings. Several different orders of the Mennonite Church have been established in Ontario, all sharing a common foundation but differing slightly in practices. In some areas, Mennonite churches were known as Missionary churches.

Location	Earliest Records	Church Still Active	Date of Existing Building	Current Name	Additional Information
Gormley	1873	yes	1931	Gormley United Missionary	Operated as a Union Church for the first ten years.
Heise Hill	1808	yes	1877	Heise Hill Brethren in Christ Church	Established by members of the Dunkard order. Services held in homes 1808-1877. Called the Markham Meeting House till 1896.
Stouffville	1903	yes	1968	Stouffville Missionary Church	In 1987 the 1903 building, which had been used for Christian Education since 1968, was demolished and a new facility built.
Oak Ridges		yes		Brethren in Christ	
Shrubmount	c.1884	no	1884		Privately owned.

SOCIETY OF FRIENDS (QUAKERS)

The Quaker influence in Whitchurch Township was centred at Newmarket and Pine Orchard. Quaker families travelling together settled parcels of land along Yonge Street north of Aurora and to the east, across the Bogarttown Sideroad (Mulock Drive/Vivian Road). The Yonge Street Friends were granted a preparative meeting in 1804 and met in members' homes until their meeting house was erected between 1808 and 1810. The Pine Orchard preparative meeting was established in 1810 and their meeting house erected in 1816. The division between the orthodox Friends and progressive Hicksites occurred in 1828, and a further schism between orthodox and conservative Quakers took place in 1881.

Location	Earliest Records	Church Still Active	Date of Existing Building	Current Name	Additional Information
Newmarket	1804	yes	1810	Yonge Street Friends House	A Hicksite meeting house was built at Armitage after the division in 1828 and later demolished. Hicksite burial ground remains.
Pine Orchard	1810	open on special occasions	1830	Pine Orchard Meeting House	The 1816 building was moved to Aurora in 1945; now a commercial building. The 1830 building (used by the Hicksites) was remodelled in 1945 and remains on the site.

BAPTIST CHURCHES

The following are Baptist churches that originated as Baptist congregations. Several other Baptist churches currently in Whitchurch-Stouffville grew from other church connections.

Location	Earliest Records	Church Still Active	Date of Existing Building	Current Name	Additional Information
Stouffville Road	1848	yes	1877	Springvale Baptist Church	Earlier names: Providence Baptist and Second Markham Baptist.
Baker Hill	1867	yes	1867	Baker Hill Baptist Church	Members originally travelled to second Markham for worship.
Stouffville	1873	yes	1925	Stouffville Baptist Church	Land for the original church was donated by Abram Stouffer in 1925; a new church was erected at a new location.

ANGLICAN CHURCHES

The majority of the Anglican churches were in towns within the Township of Whitchurch. Since the Church of England was the official faith of the British government, it was given certain privileges in Upper Canada. Over the years they proved difficult to maintain. Many changes were made during the twentieth century to accommodate members from different cultural backgrounds. The name was officially changed to the Anglican Church of Canada in 1955.

Location	Earliest Records	Church Still Active	Date of Existing Building	Current Name	Additional Information
Aurora	1843	yes	1884	Trinity Anglican Church	Congregation first met in a home; first building erected in 1846.
Oak Ridges	1848	yes		St. John's	
Stouffville	1879	yes	1961 1984 addition	Christ Church	First church built 1882 on Main Street. The 1961 building was erected at present location.
Newmarket	1820	yes	1884	St. Paul's	Regular meetings were held from 1832. The early church was built about this time. The 1884 building was declared unsafe and closed in 1992.

ROMAN CATHOLIC CHURCHES

Location	Earliest Records	Church Still Active	Date of Existing Building	Current Name	Additional Information
Newmarket	1841	yes	1979	St. John's Chrysostom	The first church was built 1855, the second in 1874.
Stouffville	1983	yes	1983	St. Mark	
Musselman's Lake	1926	no	1933		St. William's held services in summer only. The building is currently privately owned.

CHURCH OF CHRIST

The Church of Christ is a conservative body of Protestant Christians that emerged from a movement to restore the doctrines and practices of the early Christian church. Two churches were formed in Whitchurch—one in Stouffville, and the other at Pine Orchard.

Location	Earliest Records	Church Still Active	Date of Existing Building	Current Name	Additional Information
Pine Orchard	1904	yes	1916	Church of Christ	First met in a member's home, then in the Temperance Hall before the church was built.

NON-AFFILIATED CHURCHES

Location	Earliest Records	Church Still Active	Date of Existing Building	Current Name	Additional Information
Vivian		yes	1938	McCormack Memorial Church	Members met in Shrubmount school and McCormick's store prior to building the church.
Stouffville Disciple Church	c.1865	no	1868		The chapel was originally erected on the Tenth Line North and moved in 1904 to the west end of Stouffville. The congregation was dissolved in 1934; building currently privately owned.

APPENDIX B

SCHOOLS

Hillcrest School. Whitchurch-Stouffville Museum

The Township of Whitchurch was divided into thirteen rural school sections. Schools that served children in each area were numbered accordingly, that is, all students living in School Section Number One would attend S.S. #1 school. Schools also were given names related to the community where they were located, so that S.S. #1 also became known as the Hartman School, named for Hartman's Corners, where it was situated.

Union schools were established on the borders of two (or more) townships. These schools were designated U.S.S. #___, and taxes collected by these school boards were divided between the townships according to the number of children attending from each. Whitchurch had five union schools.

Little information exists on the first schools of Whitchurch Township. Many of these early schools were held sporadically, when there was a demand in the neighbourhood and when a teacher could be obtained. It was not uncommon for schools to close for several terms, then resume operating when conditions improved. Dates given in the Earliest Records column are taken from the 1850 Inspector's Report and may not be entirely accurate. Further information is available in the archives at the Whitchurch-Stouffville Museum.

School Section	Name	Earliest Record	Existing Building	Additional Information
#1	Hartman	1828	1952	Located east of Aurora on the Aurora Sideroad.
#2	Vandorf	1831	1870 1956	Two buildings remain on different sites. The 1870 one is part of the Whitchurch-Stouffville Museum. The 1956 building is now a factory.
#3	Bogarttown	1836	1857	Relocated in 1979 to form part of the Whitchurch-Stouffville Museum.
#4	Pine Orchard	1849	1924	Now privately owned.
#5	Vivian	1849	1873 1955	Two buildings remain on different sites. The 1873 building is now a private residence. The 1955 building operates as the Vivian Outdoor Education Centre.

School Section	Name	Earliest Record	Existing Building	Additional Information
#6	White Rose	1850	1948	
#7	Lloyd	1850	1903	Used by Board of Education Works Department.
#8	Hillcrest (Sixth Line)	1844	1870 1959	Two buildings remain on different sites. The 1870 building forms part of a factory. The 1959 building is a residence.
#9	Lemonville	1849	1923	Now the Lemonville Community Centre.
#10	Bloomington	1826	1898	Private residence.
#11	Ballantrae	1844	1973	The only rural school still operating on its original site; currently used by a church.
#12	Bethesda	1860	1872	
#13	Lake Wilcox	1951	1971	Still in use as a school.
U.S.S. #1	Oak Ridges	1854	1914	A union school with King Township; still operating as a school.
U.S.S. #2	Ringwood	1838	1887	A union school with Markham Township; currently used by a church.
U.S.S. #3	Armitage	1860	1910	A union school with King Township; demolished in 1990.
U.S.S. #4	Shrubmount	1878	1954	A union school with East Gwillimbury Township; now privately owned.
U.S.S. #	S.S. #11 Scott	1915	1915	A union school with Scott, Uxbridge and East Gwillimbury; now privately owned.

STOUFFVILLE SCHOOLS

Name	Earliest Record	Existing Building	Additional Information
Summitview (Stouffville Public/Stouffville Continuation School)	1841	1877	Oldest school in Stouffville.
Orchard Park	1950s	1950s	
Stouffville District Secondary School	1954	1954	Several additions.
St. Mark	1964	1965	

NEWMARKET SCHOOLS

The first schools were run by the Quakers. Classes were held at a variety of locations within the town prior to incorporation in 1858. Alexander Muir School (originally Newmarket Public School) was built in 1891 and stood for more than one hundred years.

AURORA SCHOOLS

An early school is reported in 1822. Aurora Public School (Church Street School) was built in 1886, replacing an earlier building on the site. It remains standing at time of publication, housing the Aurora Museum and other organizations.

MUNICIPAL GOVERNMENT

WHITCHURCH TOWNSHIP OFFICIALS 1825–49
Note: Spelling used is that of original documents.

YEAR	WARDEN	ASSESSOR	COLLECTOR	TOWN CLERK
1825				Wm. Barber
1826	Eli Gorham	Wm. Reader	Samuel Ball	Joseph Hewitt
	John Bogart Jr.	J. Hewitt		
1827	Eli Gorham	Wm. McCausland	Jas. Pearson	John Bogart Jr.
	John Bogart Jr.	Samuel Ball		
1828	Martin Bogart	James Pearson	Isaac Lundy	John Bogart Jr.
	Jno. Bogart Sr.	Samuel Ball		
1829	Martin Bogart	Samuel Ball	J. Willson Jr.	John Bogart Jr.
	Eli Gorham	Joseph Randall		
1830	James Faulker	Joshua Willson Jr.	Isaac Playter	John Bogart Jr.
	T. Millard	P. Bogart		
1831	Isaac Lundy	Isaac Playter	J. Willson Jr.	John Bogart Jr.
	Jacob Wiedman	Jno. Willson		
1832	Jno. Balsfred	J. Playter	James Harman	John Bogart Jr.
	Abraham Stover			

YEAR	COMMISSIONER	ASSESSOR	COLLECTOR	TOWN CLERK
1836	Jas. Pearson (C)	Isaac Hunter	J. Playter	John Bogart Jr.
	S.Pearson	J. Bogart Jr.		
	Joshua Willson			
	Lud. Wiedman			
1837	J. Pearson (C)	P. Bogart	Wm. Seton	John Bogart Jr.
	_ Macklin			
	Eli Gorham			
	Jos. Peason			

In 1838 there was no annual meeting held because the Rebellion was taking place. Township officers were to remain the same, except those that the commissioners knew to be under bond or implicated.

YEAR	WARDEN	ASSESSOR	COLLECTOR	TOWN CLERK
1839	Jos. Willson	Daniel Hunter	Thomas Roper	John Bogart Jr.
	Robert Fenton			
	J. Willson			
	Isaac Lundy			

YEAR	WARDEN	ASSESSOR	COLLECTOR	TOWN CLERK
1840	Eli Gorham (C)	Ben Pearson	William Seaton	John Bogart Jr.
	Philip Bogart			
	Jno. Miller			
	Jno. Macklin			
1841	T. Willson (C)	J. Player	William Seaton	John Bogart Jr.
	P. Bogart			
	Benj. Bozer			
	D. Hunter			
1842	B. Bozer	T. Clubine	William Seaton	John Bogart Jr.
	J. Dockler Sr.			
	T. Hunter			
1843	T. Willson (C)	William Seaton	_ Wiedman	John Bogart Jr.
	T. W. Collins			
	Jacob Clack			
	T. Bozer			
	W. Graham			
1844	P. Pearson (C)	Henry Wiedman	Henry Wiedman	John Bogart Jr.
	T. Macklin			
	J. Bozer			
	T. Botsford			
1845	M.T. Empy (C)		John Bogart Jr.	
	J. B. Collwel			
	C. Stouffer			
	H. Norman			
1846	M.T. Empy (C)			John Bogart Jr.
	T. Botsford			
	H. Widdifield			
	William Seaton			
1847	M.T. Empy (C)			John Bogart Jr.
	J. Cook			
	R.H. Smith			
	J. Patterson			
1848	J. Hewitt (C)			J. Hewitt
	T. Pearson			
	J. Doherty			
	J. Macklin			
1849	P. Pearson (C)			J. Hewitt
	J. Hunt			
	Nelson Scott			
	John Hill			

WHITCHURCH TOWNSHIP OFFICIALS 1850-1970

YEAR	REEVE	DEPUTY-REEVE	COUNCILLORS	TOWN CLERK
1850	Joseph Hartman	Henry Wideman	Sam. Pearson John Macklem Geo. Playter	Geo. Porter
1851	Joseph Hartman	Henry Wideman	Sam. Pearson John Macklem Geo. Playter	Jos. Hewitt
1852	Joseph Hartman	Henry Wideman	Geo. Playter Robt. H. Smith Geo. Brodie	Jos. Collins
1853	Joseph Hartman	Robt. H. Smith	Geo. Playter Geo. Brodie John Macklem	Jos. Collins
1854	Joseph Hartman	John R. Brown	John Macklem Geo. Playter Arden Smith	Jos. Collins
1855	Joseph Hartman	John R. Brown	Geo. Playter Sam. Pearson David March	Jos. Collins
1856	Joseph Hartman	John R. Brown	David March Joshua Willson J. Johnson	Jos. Collins
1857	Joseph Hartman	Maxson Jones	Joshua Willson Mr. Irwin Mr. Taylor	Jos. Collins
1858	Joseph Hartman	Maxson Jones	Ed. Wheeler Phil. Macklem Jos. Taylor	Jos. Collins
1859	Joseph Hartman	Maxson Jones	Jos. Taylor Phil. Macklem John Ironsides	Jos. Collins
1860	John Ironsides	Phil. Macklem	Geo. Harrison John Randall Alex. Brodie	Jos. Collins
1861	John Ironsides	Ed. Wheeler	Phil. Macklem John Randall Geo. Harrison	Jos. Collins
1862	John Ironsides	Ed. Wheeler	Robt. McCormack Phil. Macklem Geo. H. Silvester	Jos. Collins
1863	Ed. Wheeler	John Randall	Phil. Macklem Benj. Pearson Robt. McCormack	Jos. Collins
1864	Ed. Wheeler	John Randall	Phil. Macklem Robt. McCormack Geo. Harrison	Jos. Collins
1865	John Randall	Phil. Macklem	Robt. McCormack Geo. Harrison Maxson Jones	Jos. Collins

YEAR	REEVE	DEPUTY-REEVE	COUNCILLORS	TOWN CLERK
1866	John Randall	Phil. Macklem	Robt. McCormack Maxson Jones Ed. Wheeler	Jos. Collins
1867	Ed. Wheeler	Phil. Macklem	Maxson Jones Joel Baker John Clubine	Jos. Collins
1868	Ed. Wheeler	Phil. Macklem	John Randall Robt. McCormack Maxson Jones	Jos. Collins
1869	John Randall	Phil. Macklem	Robt. Smith Robt. McCormack Maxson Jones	Jos. Collins
1870	John Randall	Maxson Jones Phil. Randall	Joel Baker Robt. Smith	Jos. Collins
1871	Ed. Wheeler	Maxson Jones	Robt. McCormack Joel Baker A. Henderson	Jos. Collins
1872	John Randall	Maxson Jones Phil. Macklem	John Clubine Joel Baker	Jos. Collins
1873	John Randall	Maxson Jones Phil. Macklem	Silas Lundy Francis Boake	Jos. Collins
1874	Maxson Jones	Phil. Macklem Silas Lundy	Wm. B. Sanders Jos. C. Lundy	Jos. Collins
1875	Maxson Jones	Silas Lundy Wm. B. Sanders	Thomas Lloyd Jos. C. Lundy	Jos. Collins
1876	Maxson Jones	Jos. C. Lundy Thomas Lloyd	J. Jamieson Robt. McCormack	Jos. Collins
1877	Maxson Jones	Jos. C. Lundy Thomas Lloyd	J. Jamieson R. L. McCormack	Jos. Collins
1878	Jos. C. Lundy	Thomas Lloyd J. Jamieson	John Irwin John Miller	Jos. Collins
1879	Jos. C. Lundy	J. Jamieson Thomas Lloyd	John Irwin Lot Hartman	Jos. Collins
1880	J.C. Lundy	J. Jamieson Thomas Lloyd	John Irwin Lot Hartman	Jos. Collins
1881	J.C. Lundy	J. Jamieson Lot Hartman	John Irwin C. J. Brodie	Jos. Collins
1882	Maxson Jones	J. Jamieson Chas. J. Brodie	John Irwin Albert Bogart	Jos. Collins
1883	Maxson Jones	Chas. Brodie Lot Hartman	John Irwin J. Burkholder	Jos. Collins
1884	Maxson Jones	Chas. Brodie Lot Hartman	John Irwin J. Burkholder	Jos. Collins
1885	Maxson Jones	Chas. Brodie Lot Hartman	John Irwin J. Burkholder	Jos. Collins
1886	Chas. Brodie	Lot Hartman John Irwin	J. Burkholder Clarkson Playter	Jos. C. Lundy
1887	Chas. Brodie	Lot Hartman Clark. Playter	Geo. L. Macklem Wm. A. McCormack	Jos. C. Lundy

YEAR	REEVE	DEPUTY-REEVE	COUNCILLORS	TOWN CLERK
1888	Chas. Brodie	Lot Hartman G.L. Macklem	Seneca Baker Wm. McCormack	Jos. C. Lundy
1889	Maxson Jones	Seneca Baker Wm. McCormack	Aaron Haines Ed. Widdifield	Jos. C. Lundy
1890	Maxson Jones	Seneca Baker Wm. McCormack	J.E. Widdifield Aaron Haines	Jos. C. Lundy
1891	Maxson Jones	Seneca Baker Wm. McCormack	J.E. Widdifield Aaron Haines	Jos. C. Lundy
1892	Wm. McCormack	Seneca Baker J.E. Widdifield	Aaron Haines Lemon Baker	Jos. C. Lundy
1893	Wm. McCormack	Seneca Baker J. Widdifield	Aaron Haines Lemon Baker	Jos. C. Lundy
1894	Wm. McCormack	Seneca Baker Aaron Haines	Lemon Baker A. Bogart	Jos. C. Lundy
1895	Seneca Baker	Aaron Haines Lemon Baker	Albert Bogart John Scott	Jos. C. Lundy
1896	Seneca Baker	Aaron Haines Lemon Baker	Albert Bogart T.D. Skinner	Jos. C. Lundy
1897	Aaron Haines	Lemon Baker Albert Bogart	Geo. H. Powell T.D. Skinner	Jos. C. Lundy
1898	Aaron Haines	Lemon Baker Geo. H. Powell	Wm. H. Clark Charles Case	Jos. C. Lundy
1899	Aaron Haines		Lemon Baker Wm. H. Clark Geo. H. Powell T.D. Skinner	Jos. C. Lundy
1900	Aaron Haines		Lemon Baker Geo. H. Powell Wm. H. Clark T.D. Skinner	Jos. C. Lundy
1901	Lemon Baker		Wm. H. Clark S.P. Foote Wm. McDonald R.T. Soules	Jos. C. Lundy
1902	Aaron Haines		S.P. Foote Wm. McDonald Wm. H. Clark R.T. Soules	Jos. C. Lundy
1903	Lemon Baker		Wm. H. Clark	Jos. C. Lundy
1904	Lemon Baker		R.T. Soules Wm. Leathers T.D. Skinner Sm. Thompson	Jos. C. Lundy
1905	R.T. Soules		Wm. Leathers S.P. Foote Wm. Thompson D. Rusnell	Jos. C. Lundy
1906	R.T. Soules		D.H. Rusnell S.P. Foote Wm. Thompson T.D. Skinner	Jos. C. Lundy
1907	Seneca Baker	S.P. Foote	W.H. Clark T.J. Spaulding Wm. Thompson	Jos. C. Lundy
1908	Seneca Baker	S.P. Foote	W.H. Clark Wm. Thompson T. Spaulding	Jos. C. Lundy
1909	S.P. Foote	W.H. Clark	C.W. Playter J.W. Grose Wm. Thompson	Jos. C. Lundy
1910	S.P. Foote	W.H. Clark	C.W. Playter W.J. Grose Wm. Thompson	Jos. C. Lundy
1911	S.P. Foote	W.H. Clark	H. Widdifield Wm. Thompson T.J. Spaulding	Jos. C. Lundy
1912	W.H. Clark	T.J. Spaulding	H. Widdifield Thos. Moorehead D.H. Rusnell	Jos. C. Lundy
1913	Seneca Baker	T. Spaulding	T. Moorehead D.H. Rusnell F. Legge	W.H. Clark
1914	Seneca Baker	T. Spaulding	D.H. Rusnell T. Moorehead Frank Legge	W.H. Clark
1915	T. Spaulding D.H. Rusnell	T. Moorehead	F.A. Legge	W.H. Clark
1916	T. Spaulding	T. Moorehead	Gideon Baker F.A. Legge D.H. Rusnell	W.H. Clark
1917	T. Spaulding	T. Moorehead	F.A. Legge G.G. Baker D.H. Rusnell	W.H. Clark
1918	T. Spaulding	T. Moorehead	G.G. Baker F.A. Legge D.H. Rusnell	W.H. Clark
1919	S.P. Foote	D.H. Rusnell	G.G. Baker Wm. Crawford J.A. Mabley	W.H. Clark
1920	D.H. Rusnell	Wm. Crawford	J.A. Mabley Morgan Baker R.E. Ratcliff	W.H. Clark
1921	Wm. Crawford	Morgan Baker	R.E. Ratcliff Herman Kidd	W.H. Clark

YEAR	REEVE	DEPUTY-REEVE	COUNCILLORS	TOWN CLERK	YEAR	REEVE	DEPUTY-REEVE	COUNCILLORS	TOWN CLERK
1922	Wm. Crawford	Morgan Baker	Geo. H. Leary Geo. H. Leary E. Dennis A.M. Baker	W.H. Clark	1938	C.E. Toole	Jess Cook	Geo. H. Leary H. Kidd H.Wells	John W. Crawford
1923	Wm. Crawford	Morgan Baker	Geo. H. Leary Edgar Dennis A.M. Baker	W.H. Clark	1939	C.E. Toole	Jess Cook	Geo. H. Leary H. Kidd H.Wells	John W. Crawford
1924	Morgan Baker	Geo. H. Leary	A.M. Baker C.E. Dennis H. Kidd	W.H. Clark	1940	C.E. Toole	Jesse Cook	Geo. H. Leary H. Kidd H.Wells	John W. Crawford
1925	Morgan Baker	Geo. H. Leary	A.M. Baker C.E. Dennis H. Kidd	W.H. Clark	1941	C.E. Toole	Jess Cook (died) Geo. Leary	Geo. Leary H. Kidd H.Wells (Ed. Logan) (Eugene Baker)	John W. Crawford
1926	Morgan Baker	Geo. H. Leary	A.M. Baker H. Kidd Wm. Crawford	Hugh W. Clark (pro-tem)	1942	C.E. Toole	Geo. H. Leary	E. Baker Ed. Logan L.P. Evans	John W. Crawford
1927	Morgan Baker	Herman Kid	Wm. Crawford R.E. Ratcliff G.W. Williams	Hugh W. Clark	1943	Geo. H. Leary	L.P. Evans	Ed. Logan E. Baker L.J. Harper	John W. Crawford
1928	Morgan Baker	Herman Kidd	Wm. Crawford R.E. Ratcliff G.W. William	Hugh W. Clark	1944	Geo. H. Leary	L.P. Evans	Ed. Logan E. Baker L.J. Harper	John W. Crawford
1929	Herman Kidd R.E. Ratcliff	G.W. William	L.P. Evans Newton Rae	Wm. Crawford	1945	Geo. H. Leary	L.P. Evans	Ed. Logan L.J. Harper Ivan McLaughlin	John W. Crawford
1930	Herman Kidd	G.W. William	L.P. Evans R.E. Ratcliff Newton Rae	Wm. Crawford	1946	L.P. Evans	Ed. Logan	L.J. Harper Ivan McLaughlin F. Timbers	John W. Crawford
1931	Herman Kidd	G.W. William	R.E. Ratcliff L.P. Evans Newton Rae	Wm. Crawford (H. Kidd) pro-tem	1947	L.P. Evans	Ed. Logan	L.J. Harper Ivan McLaughlin F. Timbers	John W. Crawford
1932	Herman Kidd	Newton Rae	C.E. Toole R.E. Ratcliff I. N. Morton	Herman Kidd	1948	L.P. Evans	Ed. Logan	L.J. Harper Ivan McLaughlin Fred Timbers	John W. Crawford
1933	Herman Kidd	Newton Rae	C.E. Toole R.E. Ratcliff I.N. Morton	Herman Kidd	1949	Ed. Logan	I. McLaughlin	P.S. Legge F. Timbers R.C. Baycroft	L.J. Harper (deputy-clerk)
1934	Herman Kidd	Newton Rae	C.E. Toole R.E. Ratcliffe I.N. Morton	John Crawford (pro-tem)	1950	Ed. Logan	I. McLaughlin	F. Timbers P.S. Legge R.C. Baycroft	John W. Crawford L.J. Harper (deputy-clerk)
1935	Newton Rae	C.E. Toole	Jess Cook Geo. H. Leary L.P. Evans	John W. Crawford	1951	I. McLaughlin	F. Timbers	R.C. Baycroft P.S. Legge E.L. McCarron	John W. Crawford
1936	Newton Rae	C.E. Toole	Geo. H. Leary L.P. Evans Jess Cook	John W. Crawford	1952	I. McLaughlin	F. Timbers	R.C. Baycroft E.L. McCarron Delos Graham	John W. Crawford
1937	C.E. Toole	Jess Cook	Geo. H. Leary H.Wells Herman Kidd	John W. Crawford					

137

YEAR	REEVE	DEPUTY-REEVE	COUNCILLORS	TOWN CLERK
1953	I. McLaughlin	F. Timbers	P.S. Legge E.L. McCarron Delos Graham	J.W. Crawford
1954	I. McLaughlin	F. Timbers	P.S. Legge E.L. McCarron Delos Graham	J.W. Crawford
1955	I. McLaughlin	P.S. Legge	G.E. Richardson C. Wallwork Delos Graham	J.W. Crawford
1956	P.S. Legge	G.E. Richardson	C. Wallwork Frank Williams Delos Graham	J.W. Crawford
1957	P.S. Legge	G.E. Richardson	F. Williams C. Wallwork J.C. Wylie	J.W. Crawford
1958	P.S. Legge	G.E. Richardson	C. Wallwork F. Williams Elsie Gibbs	J.W. Crawford
1959	G.E. Richardson	C. Wallwork	F. Williams Elsie Gibbs R. Farquharsonn	J.W. Crawford
1960	G.E. Richardson	C. Wallwork	F. Williams I. McLaughlin R. Farquharsonn	J.W. Crawford
1961	Clifford Wallwork	F. William	R. Farquharsonn Ivan McLaughlin Elsie Gibbs	John W. Crawford
1962	Clifford Wallwork	F. Williams	R. Farquharson Ivan McLaughlin Elsie Gibbs	John W. Crawford
1963	F. Williams	R. Farquharson	S. Burnett Alvin S. Farmer Ivan McLaughlin	John W. Crawford
1964	F. Williams	R. Farquharson	S. Burnett Alvin S. Farmer Ivan McLaughlin	Thos. Kerr
1965	R. Farquharson	S. Burnet	Alvin S. Farmer James P.Smith Ivan McLaughlin	Thos. Kerr
1966	R. Farquharson	S. Burnet	Ivan McLaughlin Frank Williams Henry Nauta	Thos. Kerr
1967	R. Farquharson	S. Burnet	Ivan McLaughlin Frank Williams Henry Nauta	Thos. Kerr
1968	S. Burnet	Lawrence Hennessey	Norman Barnard Betty Van Nostrand Robt. S. Lewis	Thos. Kerr
1969	S. Burnet	Lawrence C. Hennessey	Norman Barnard B. Van Nostrand Robt. S. Lewis	Thos. Kerr
1970	S. Burnet	Norman Barnard	Melvyn Baker Gordon Ratcliff B. Van Nostrand	Thos. Kerr

VILLAGE OF STOUFFVILLE OFFICIALS 1877-1970

YEAR	REEVE	DEPUTY-REEVE	COUNCILLORS	TOWN CLERK
1877	James Dougherty			
1878	James Dougherty			
1879	E. Wheler			H.W. Woodgate
1880	E. Wheler			H.W. Woodgate
1881	James Dougherty			H.W. Woodgate
1882	James Dougherty			H.W. Woodgate
1883	W.B. Sanders			H.W. Woodgate
1884	W.B. Sanders			H.W. Woodgate
1885	W.B. Sanders			H.W. Woodgate
1886	W.B. Sanders			H.W. Woodgate
1887	W.B. Sanders			H. S. Woodgate (Warden York Co.)
1888	W.B. Sanders			H.W. Woodgate
1889	W.B. Sanders			H.W. Woodgate
1890	R.J. Dale			H.W. Woodgate
1891	R.J. Dale			H.W. Woodgate
1892	R.J. Dale			H.W. Woodgate
1893	W.B. Sanders			H.W. Woodgate
1894	Hiram Johnson			H.W. Woodgate
1895	Hiram Johnson			H.W. Woodgate
1896	Hiram Johnson			H.W. Woodgate
1897	James Ratcliff			H.W. Woodgate
1898	James Ratcliff			H.W. Woodgate
1899	W.J. Stark			H.W. Woodgate
1900	W.J. Stark			H.W. Woodgate
1901	J.L. Baker			H.W. Woodgate
1902	J.L. Baker J.A. Todd			H.W. Woodgate
1903	R. Underhill			H.W. Woodgate
1904	R. Underhill			H.W. Woodgate
1905	James McCullough			H.W. Woodgate
1906	Dr. W.A. Sangster			J. Urquhart
1907	Dr. W.A. Sangster			J. Urquhart
1908	R.P. Coulson			J. Urquhart
1909	R.P. Coulson			J. Urquhart
1910	R.P. Coulson			J. Urquhart
1911	R.P. Coulson			J. Urquhart
1912	R.P. Coulson			J. Urquhart

YEAR	REEVE	DEPUTY-REEVE	COUNCILLORS	TOWN CLERK
1913	Dr. W.A. Sangster			J. Urquhart
1914	Dr. W.A. Sangster			J. Urquhart
1915	Dr. W.A. Sangster			J. Urquhart
1916	Dr. W.A. Sangster			J. Urquhart
1917	J.H. Ratcliff			J. Urquhart
1918	J.H. Ratcliff			J. Urquhart
1919	J.H. Ratcliff			J. Urquhart
1920	J.H. Ratcliff			J. Urquhart
1921	J.H. Ratcliff			J. Urquhart
1922	A.H. Lehman		W.E. Morden / A.W. Scott / Geo. Lee / F. Silversides	J. Urquhart
1923	W.E. Morden		F. Silversides / AW. Scott / B.E. Beebe / G.H. Lee	J. Urquhart
1924	J.S. Dougherty		E. Lunau / F. Silvester / F.A. Dales / F. Silversides	J. Urquhart
1925	F.W. Silvester		F.W. Silversides / Jos. Borinsky / H.W. Sanders / J. Cleaver	J. Urquhart
1926	F.W. Silvester		Jos. Borinsky / J.W. Cleaver / H.W. Sanders / W. Brillinger	J. Urquhart
1927	F.W. Silvester		H.W. Sanders / MacKinnon / D. Rusnell	J.S. Dougherty
1928	H.W. Sanders		Jos. Borinsky / Geo. Dowswell / J. MacKinnon / A.J. Ward	J.S. Dougherty
1929	H.W. Sanders		D.H. Rusnell / F.C. Rowbotham / Jos. Borinsky / A.J. Ward	J.S. Dougherty
1930	H.W. Sanders		Jos. Borinsky / A.J. Ward / D.H. Rusnell / F.C. Rowbotham	J.S. Dougherty
1931	W.E. Morden		A.E. Weldon / M.E. Watts / G. Dowswell / D.H. Rusnell	J.S. Dougherty
1932	W.E. Morden		A.E. Weldon / M.E. Watts / G. Dowswell / D.H. Rusnell	J.S. Dougherty
1933	W.E. Morden		D.H. Rusnell / G. Dowswell / M.W. Watts / A.E. Weldon	J.S. Dougherty
1934	H.W. Sanders		A.E. Weldon / M.E. Watts / R. Brown / W. Brillinger	J.S. Dougherty
1935	H.W. Sanders		A.E. Weldon / M.E. Watts / R. Brown / W. Brillinger	J.S. Dougherty
1936	H.W. Sanders			J.S. Dougherty
1937	A.E. Weldon		W.C. Brillinger / Ira D. Rusnell / R.E. Brown / T.A. Swift	J.S. Dougherty
1938	A.E. Weldon		R.E. Brown / M. Tait / I.D. Rusnell / J.H. Silverthorn	J.S. Dougherty
1939	A.E. Weldon		R.E. Brown / I.D. Rusnell / J.H. Silverthorn / D. Holden	J.S. Dougherty
1940	A.E. Weldon		R.E. Brown / D. Rusnell / J.H. Silverthorn / D. Holden	J.S. Dougherty
1941	A.E. Weldon		Hugh Boyd / I.D. Rusnell / J.H. Silverthorn / Ross E. Brown	Geo. J. Storey
1942	A.E. Weldon		Hugh Boyd / I.D. Rusnell / J.H. Silverthorn / Ross E. Brown	Geo. J. Storey
1943	A.E. Weldon		H. Boyd / J.H. Silverthorn / A.V. Nolan / Wm. F. Ratcliff	Geo. J. Storey
1944	A.E. Weldon		H. Boyd / R.E. Brown / W.C. Brillinger / A.V. Nolan	Geo. J. Storey

YEAR	REEVE	DEPUTY-REEVE	COUNCILLORS	TOWN CLERK
1945	A.V. Nolan		H. Boyd / R.E. Brown / E.A. Button / John W. Smits	Geo. J. Storey
1946	A.V. Nolan		H. Boyd / R.E. Brown / E.A. Button / John W. Smits	Geo. J. Storey
1947	A.V. Nolan		H. Boyd / Chas. H. Bell / J.W. Smits / F.C. Rowbotham	Geo. J. Storey
1948	A.V. Nolan		Clayton Baker / Henry Ogden / G. Ratcliff / J. Scott	Geo. J. Storey
1949	A.V. Nolan		Clayton Baker / Henry Ogden / G. Ratcliff / J. Scott	Geo. J. Storey
1950	A.V. Nolan / Henry Ogden		Clayton Baker / Henry Ogden / F.G. Ratcliff / Harry Ratcliff	Geo. J. Storey
1951	Henry Ogden		F.G. Ratcliff / H.F. Ratcliff / H. Spofford / Reg. Stouffe	Geo. J. Storey
1952	Henry Ogden		H.R. Murphy / F.G. Ratcliff / H.F. Ratcliff / Reg. Stouffe	Garfield D. Brown
1953	Henry Ogden		Del. Booth / Milton Burk / Elmer Daniels / F.G. Ratcliff	Garfield D. Brown
1954	Henry Ogden		F.G. Ratcliff / Elmer Daniels / Del. Booth / Milton Burk	Garfield D. Brown
1955	Elmer Daniels			
1956	Elmer Daniels			
1957	Elmer Daniels			
1958	Elmer Daniels			
1959	Gar. Lehman			
1960	Gar. Lehman			
1961	K. Wagg	K. Laushway	G. Lehman / Wm. S. Parsons / Henry Slack	R.E. Corner
1962	W. Timber	K. Laushway	G. Lehman / Wm. S. Parsons / Norman Span	R.E. Corner
1963	W. Timbers	K. Laushway	Wm. G. Parsons / K.W. Betz / Norman Span	R.E. Corner
1964	W. Timbers	K. Laushway	K.W. Betz / Wm. S. Parsons / Norman Span	R.E. Corner
1965	W. Timbers	K. Laushway	K.W. Betz / Wm. S. Parsons / Norman Span	R.E. Corner
1966	K. Laushway	Wm. S. Parsons	Thos. Lonergan / Robt. S. Lewis / Jas. McKellar	R.E. Corner
1967	K. Laushway	Wm. S. Parsons	Thos. Lonergan / Robt. S. Lewis / Jas. McKellar	R.E. Corner
1968	K. Laushway	Wm. S. Parsons	Thos. Lonergan / Jas. McKellar / Ethel Mole	R.E. Corner
1969	K. Laushway	Wm. S. Parsons	Thos. Lonergan / Jas. McKellar / Ethel Mole	R.E. Corner
1970	K. Laushway	Jas. McKellar	Ian Chapman / Thos. Lonergan / Ethel Mole	R.E. Corner

TOWN OF WHITCHURCH-STOUFFVILLE OFFICIALS 1971-1993

YEAR	REEVE	DEPUTY-REEVE	COUNCILLORS	TOWN CLERK
1971	K. Laushway		B. VanNostrand / H. Simpson / M. Baker / G. Ratcliff / June Button / Thos. Lonergan	R.E. Corner / E. Foskett (deputy-clerk)
1972	G. Ratcliff		A. Starr / J. Wong / M. Baker / C. Joice / J. Button / E. King	
1974	G. Ratcliff		A. Starr / R. Wedley	

YEAR	REEVE	DEPUTY-REEVE	COUNCILLORS	TOWN CLERK
			M. Baker	
			C. Joice	
			J. Button	
			E. King	
1976	G. Ratcliff		J. Doble	
			R. Wedley	
			Wm. McNalley	
			C. Wm. Kamps	
			J. Button	
			J. Sanders	
1978	Eldred King		J. Doble	
			R. Wedley	
			Wm. McNalley	
			C. Wm. Kamps	
			J. Button	
			J. Sanders	
1980	Eldred King		C.E. Warden	
			T. Wood	
			Jas. N. Rae	
			C. Wm. Kamps	
			W. Morley	
			J. Sanders	
1982	Eldred King (1984-T. Wood)		M. Marshall	
			T. Wood (R. Robb)	
			Jas. N. Rae	
			F. Sainsbury	
			W. Morley	
			J. Sanders	
1985	F. Sainsbury		M. Marshall	
			R. Robb	
			Jas. N. Rae	
			W. Emmerson	
			W. Morley	
			J. Sanders	
1988	F. Sainsbury		M. Marshall	
			R. Robb	
			N. Tatone	
			W. Emmerson	
			D. Alles	
			J. Sanders (1991-S. Bellerby)	
1991	F. Sainsbury		I. Bradley	
			S. Bellerby	
			N. Tatone	
			C. Dunkeld	
			B. Ancheril	
			K. Prentice	

POST OFFICES

POST OFFICE	POSTMASTER	DATE APPOINTED	DATE VACATED
AURORA	Charles Doane	1854	9-1-1882
established 6-7-1846			
BALLANTRAE	James DeGeer	1-8-1858	7-2-1862
established 1-8-1858	Richard L. Macey	1-4-1863	30-4-1865
closed 30-11-1949	Edward Gray	1-9-1865	9-11-1866
	Isaac Lepard	1-4-1867	24-12-1868
	Daniel Prior	1-3-1869	5-5-1871
	Robert Hill	1-10-1871	1901
	Mrs. Eliza Hill	1-6-1901	7-7-1902
	W.H. Jones	1-8-1902	18-6-1913
	John Gray	14-7-1913	30-7-1923
	Gilbert Wright	15-8-1923	20-10-1949
	Mrs. Muriel Wright	24-10-1949	closed
BETHESDA	Hezekiah Pretty	1-4-1874	Nov. 1874
established 1-4-1874	Fred Pretty	1-1-1875	28-11-1887
closed 29-2-1924	David Pretty	1-3-1888	14-2-1898
	David Heise	1-4-1898	12-12-1904
	Abel T. Cayler	5-2-1905	15-11-1910
	W.H. Lever	31-1-1911	23-12-1912
	Chas. Sanderson	6-3-1913	29-10-1915
	Mrs. Alice Sanderson	6-3-1916	5-1-1924
BLOOMINGTON	S. Patterson	1-7-1863	22-7-1870
established 1-7-1863	Maxson Jones	1-1-1871	9-2-1895
closed 30-4-1920	Barton Ward	11-2-1907	2-1-1910
	Everett Barnes	15-4-1912	30-12-1919
CEDAR VALLEY	Henry Widdifield	1-3-1908	31-8-1923
	Frank Widdifield	1-10-1923	Aug. 1945
established 1-3-1908	Archibald Bolton	10-9-1945	11-1-1962
	Mrs. Hilda Bolton	25-2-1963	8-9-1964
	Mrs. Earla Brammer	29-10-1964	
GORMLEY	James Gormley	6-6-1851	16-11-1876
	Richard Lewis	1-1-1877	Feb. 1893

POST OFFICE	POSTMASTER	DATE APPOINTED	DATE VACATED
established 6-6-1851	Colin McKenzie	1-4-1883	25-1-1904
	Robert Johnson	1-3-1904	2-11-1910
	C.H. Keys	30-11-1910	15-9-1915
still active	John W. Wilson	15-9-1915	24-8-1918
	Ellis J. Webb	15-12-1918	7-1-1923
	Samuel Doner	25-4-1923	15-2-1954
	Charles Milsted	1-4-1954	24-12-1964
	Evelyn Milsted	23-2-1965	
HARTMAN established 1-11-1863 closed 1-7-1884	David Terry	1-11-1863	1877
	Hugh Campbell	28-2-1878	1879
	Mrs. Hugh Campbell	1-10-1879	12-7-1880
LEMONVILLE	John Anderson	6-11-1852	24-1-1854
	Abner Lemon	1-3-1854	8-8-1854
established 6-11-1852 closed 30-9-1937	Sam Dougherty	1-1-1855	24-10-1855
	John Hill	1-2-1856	18-1-1870
	Adam Hasting	1-3-1870	2-3-1873
	W.L. White	1-4-1873	16-11-1903
	Gideon G. Baker	1-3-1904	20-3-1912
	Miss M. White	31-3-1912	3-7-1916
	E.J. Barkey	8-8-1916	27-4-1937
MUSSELMAN'S LAKE	Mrs. Eileen Rilley	1-7-1933	16-5-1940
established 1-7-1933 closed 30-8-1969	James Pidgeon	25-6-1940	9-9-1956
	Stewart Patrick	1-5-1957	
NEWMARKET established 1822	W.B. Robinson	1822	1837
	William Roe	1837	Apr. 1879
OAK RIDGES	A. McKechnie	6-7-1851	2-9-1859
	Frederick Suttle	1-3-1860	July 1867
established 6-7-1851	O. Gregory	1-10-1867	19-11-1868
	Frank Johns	1-2-1869	24-9-1869
still active	Edwin Gorham	1-1-1870	10-9-1870
	Edward Curtis	1-1-1871	1879
	George Harker	1-1-1880	1889
	Peter Routledge	1-12-1889	20-1-1914
	John Routledge	26-2-1914	1-5-1922
	Ivan E. Scott	30-11-1922	27-4-1925
	John Blain	23-5-1925	20-10-1942
	Richard S. March	27-10-1942	

POST OFFICE	POSTMASTER	DATE APPOINTED	DATE VACATED
	Miss Elizabeth Blain	16-11-1942	
	John Blain Topper	26-3-1945	28-11-1947
	Paul E. Bishop	1-12-1947	13-3-1951
	Aneta Lockhart	2-4-1951	
	Edward C. Hawman	26-10-1951	31-3-1968
	Edwin A. Bunn	1-4-1968	
PINE ORCHARD established 1-5-1853 closed 1914	Moses Willson	1-5-1853	23-3-1859
	George Sexsmith	31-5-1859	26-10-1859
	C. Randall	1-4-1862	28-12-1872
	Nelson May	1-7-1874	1913
PLEASANTVILLE established 23-3-1908 closed 31-12-1914	Dan Lundy	23-3-1908	17-6-1908
	Nelson Collingwood	15-11-1908	31-12-1914
RINGWOOD established 1-1-1857 closed 31-1-1975	George N. Sylvester	1-1-1857	12-9-1900
	A.W. Lehman	1-11-1900	9-11-1916
	J.M. Grove	10-7-1917	2-4-1930
	Roy B. Grove	24-3-1940	29-1-1955
	Mrs. Wahneita Grove	3-2-1955	2-6-1955
	George K. Phillips	19-10-1955	31-1-1975
SHRUBMOUNT established 1-6-1884 closed 16-9-1892	Francis Boake	1-6-1884	25-2-1888
	Thos. Doyle	1-2-1890	14-3-1892
VANDORF established 1-9-1887 closed 30-4-1931	George H. Powell	1-9-1887	21-12-1910
	Alfred G. Snider	14-1-1911	30-4-1931
VIVIAN established 1-12-1866 closed 31-3-1924	George Sexsmith	1-12-1866	30-12-1867
	Robt. McCormick	1-5-1868	13-3-1907
	George L. Cox	1-11-1908	14-3-1910
	Charles McQuain	1-5-1910	28-5-1912
	George W. McCormick	1-6-1912	1-3-1924
WHITE ROSE established 1-7-1863 closed 31-3-1914	B. Pearson	1-7-1863	23-?-1864
	Jared Lloyd	1-12-1864	19-6-1887
	Stephen Wallace	1-7-1887	17-10-1890
	J.W. Johnston	1-2-1891	6-2-1892
	H.P. Smith	1-8-1892	9-10-1896
	S.T. Brooks	16-11-1896	27-1-1899

POST OFFICE	POSTMASTER	DATE APPOINTED	DATE VACATED
	Jonathan Miller	1-3-1899	6-11-1903
	Hugh Evans	1-1-1904	19-11-1906
	Wm. J. Woodcock	1-1-1912	20-8-1913
STOUFFVILLE	Charles D. Sheldon	1832	1835
	W.H. Doyle	1835	1837
	closed	1838	1841
established 1832	John Boyer	1841	
	Andrew C. Lloyd	1852	
	Edward Wheeler	1854	
still active	Samuel Fenton	1856	
	John White	1861	1864
	Edward Wheeler	1865	
	William B. Sanders	1878	1912
	Joseph A. Todd	1912	1913
	J.J. Rae	1914	1926
	E.B. Learens	1927	1945
	J. Sanders	1945	1964
	George Collins	1973	
	Gary Fisher	1974	1990
	David Glover	1990	

APPENDIX E

SUMMARY OF FOREST PRODUCTS—1871 CENSUS

	Type of Product	Amount
1.	Cubic feet of squared pine logs	900
2.	Cubic feet of squared hickory logs	1000
3.	Cubic feet of other squared timber	700
4.	Number of standard white pine logs	400
5.	Number of spruce logs	10
6.	Cords of tanbark	30
7.	Cords of fuel wood	1725

SUMMARY OF SAWMILL STATISTICS — 1861 CENSUS

NAME	DESIGN-ATION	CAPITAL INVESTED	NUMBER OF MALE HANDS	COST/ MONTH OF MALE HANDS	PRODUCTION	ANNUAL VALUE OF PRODUCTS	MOTIVE POWER	LOCATION
Alexander McKechnie	Sawyer	$3,000.	6	$80.	2000 bd. ft. per day	$4,800.	steam	lot 68, conc. 1
Dr. John Nash Eugene Nash (operated with grist mill)	Physician	$16,000.	5	$100.	170,000 bd. ft. annually	$1,400.	steam	lot 93, conc. 1
Peter Brillinger	Sawmill Owner	$1,400.	3	$30.	1,000 bd. ft. per day	$2,000	water	lot 1, conc. 4
Peter Brillinger	Sawmill Owner	$1,400.	3	$30.	1,000 bd. ft. per day	$3,000	water	lot 1, conc. 4
Israel Clubine	Sawmill Owner	$1,000.	1	$10.	50,000 bd. ft. annually	$750.	water	lot 1, conc. 4
Geo. Harrison John Van Nostrand	Sawmill Owners	$4,000.	5 (1 female)	$50.	5,000 bd. ft. per day	$15,000.	steam	lot 17, conc. 4
Thomas Lewis	Sawyer	$10,000.	1 to 11	$30.	4,000 bd. ft. per day	$1,000.	steam	lot 1, conc. 5
Samuel Dick	Sawyer	$500.	1	$10.	25,000 bd. ft. per day	$125.	water	lot ??, conc. 5
Phillip Cook	Sawyer	$1,500.	1	$10.		$360.	water	lot , conc. 6
John Isaac Gordon	Sawyer	$1,400.	3	$50.	300,000 bd. ft. annually	$750.	steam	lot ??, conc. 5
Abraham Taylor	Sawyer	$500.	1	$10.	120,000 bd. ft. annually	$2,000.	water	lot 30, conc. 6
Jacob Taylor	Farmer		Mill Not Working					
Robert Heasty Robt. McCormick	Sawyer	$1,500.	2	$38.	400,000 bd. ft. annually	$2,000.	steam	lot 29, conc. 7
Robt. McCormick James Simpson	Sawyer	$1,500.	2	$38.	500,000 bd. ft. annually	$750.	steam	lot 29, conc. 7
James Brodie (John Baker)	Sawyer	$1,000.	1	$14.	450,000 bd. ft. annually	$2,700.	steam	lot 9, conc. 8

NAME	DESIGN-ATION	CAPITAL INVESTED	NUMBER OF MALE HANDS	COST/ MONTH OF MALE HANDS	PRODUCTION	ANNUAL VALUE OF PRODUCTS	MOTIVE POWER	LOCATION
Charles Appleton	Sawyer	$1,000.	2	$30.	80,000 bd. ft. annually	$900.	steam	lot 18, conc. 8
A. Sangster	Sawmill Operator	$400.	1	$10.	50,000 bd. ft. annually	$250.	water	lot 8, conc. 9
Frederick Johnson	Sawyer	$6,000.	2	$24.	25,000 bd. ft. annually	$1,200.	steam	lot 20, conc. 9
Arthur Stapleton	Sawyer	$6,000.	2	$20.	25,000 bd. ft. annually	$1,200.	steam	lot 22, conc. 9

BIBLIOGRAPHY

CHAPTER 1: The Native People

Barkey, Jean, comp. *A Pictorial History of a Prosperous Ontario Community, Stouffville: 1877–1977.* Stouffville: The Bryant Press, 1977.

Carter, Terry. Newmarket, Ontario. Interview, 1978.

Cruikshank, E.A., ed. *The Correspondence of Lieut. Governor John Simcoe.* Vol. 3. Toronto: Ontario Historical Society, 1925.

Dibb, Gordon C. "Late Palaeo-Indian Settlement Patterns Along the Margins of the Simcoe Lowlands in Southcentral Ontario." M.A. Thesis, Department of Anthropology, Trent University, Peterborough, 1985.

Gentilcore, L, and C.G. Head. *Ontario History in Maps.* Toronto: University of Toronto Press, 1984.

Johnston, Richard B. "Archaeology of the Serpent Mounds Site." *Royal Ontario Museum, Art and Archaeology Occasional Paper 10,* 1968.

National Museums Canada. 12437 - (R)H1/400/[1850]Section E, de Rottenburg map.

Smith, Donald B. "The Dispossession of the Mississauga Indians: a Missing Chapter in the Early History of Upper Canada." In *Ontario History,* June 1981, 90.

Trewhella, Ethel Wilson. *History of the Town of Newmarket.* N.p., n.d.

van Nostrand, Dr. F.H. "Vandorf, Prehistoric and Early Historic Times: Land, Water, Trees and People." N.d.

CHAPTER 2: From Whitchurch to Whitchurch-Stouffville

Annette, Sister M., CPS. *Salute to Canada.* Oak Ridges: Our Lady of the Annunciation School, 1967.

Barkey, Jean, comp. *A Pictorial History of a Prosperous Ontario Community, Stouffville: 1877-1977.* Stouffville: The Bryant Press, 1977.

Byers, Mary, Jan Kennedy, Margaret McBurney, and the Junior League of Toronto. *Rural Roots.* Toronto: University of Toronto Press, 1976.

Historical Sketch of Whitchurch-Stouffville. Centennial Celebration of Municipal Government 1850–1950. Township of Whitchurch, 1950.

History of Toronto and County of York, Ontario. Vol. I. Toronto: C. Blackett Robinson, 1885.

Illustrated Historical Atlas of the County of York. Selected and reprinted from the original 1878 edition. Toronto: Peter Martin Associates, Ltd., 1969.

Insights. Local and Regional Government in York Region. York Region: The Municipality of the Region of York, 1981; reprinted., York Region, ca. 1987.

Mitchell, John. *The Settlement of York County.* York County: The Municipal Corporation of the County of York, 1950.

Richardson, Marjorie E. "A 'Quick' History of Whitchurch Township." 1975.

———. "Brief Sketch of the History of the Township of Whitchurch." N.d.

———. "Whitchurch Township—County—York." N.d.

A Summary of the Historical Development of York Region. York Region: Regional Municipality of York, Regional Official Plan Technical Appendix 1, June 1974.

The Town of Whitchurch-Stouffville 'A Planning Study.' An Appendix to the Official Plan. Prepared by Macroplan Ltd., Planning Consultants, 568 Lawrence Avenue West, Suite 106, Toronto, Ontario, n.d.

CHAPTER 3: From Pit-saw to Pine Plantations

Barkey, Jean. Stouffville, Ontario. Interview. February 1992.

Champion, Isabel, ed. *Markham 1793–1900.* Markham: Markham Historical Society, 1979.

Champion, Mary B., ed. *Markham Remembered.* Markham: Markham District Historical Society, 1988.

Evergreen Challenge—The Agreement Forest Story. Ontario Ministry of Natural Resources Publication, 1982.

Historical Sketch of Whitchurch-Stouffville. Centennial Celebration of Municipal Government 1850-1950. Township of Whitchurch, 1950.

History of Toronto and County of York, Ontario. Vol. II. Toronto: C. Blackett Robinson, 1885.

Hollidge, Cliff. Interview. March 1992.

Mitchell, John. *The Settlement of York County.* York County: The Municipal Corporation of the County of York, 1950.

Ratcliff, Terry. Markham, Ontario. Interview. November 1991.

Richardson, Marjorie E. "Century Farms of Whitchurch-Stouffville." April 1967.

———. Personal Notes. N.d.

———. "Vandorf Then and Now." 1979.

Rosen, Michael. Management Forester, Ministry of Natural Resources. Personal Notes. N.d.

Todd, Eleanor. *Burrs and Blackberries.* Goodwood: Eleanor Todd, 1980.

Trewhella, Ethel Wilson. *History of the Town of Newmarket.* N.p., n.d.

The Town of Whitchurch-Stouffville 'A Planning Study.' An Appendix to the Official Plan. Prepared by Macroplan Ltd., Planning Consultants, 568 Lawrence Avenue West, Suite 106, Toronto, Ontario, n.d.

The Upper Holland Conservation Report. Ontario Department of Planning and Development, 1953.

van Nostrand, Dr. F.H. Personal Notes. N.d.

van Nostrand, Dr. Peter and Janet. Vandorf, Ontario. Interview. February 1992.

CHAPTER 4: The Communities of Whitchurch

Oak Ridges, Bond Lake, Lake Wilcox, French Settlement

Annette, Sister M., CPS. *Salute to Canada.* Oak Ridges: Our Lady of the Annunciation School, 1967.

Des Rivières, D. *Exploring Richmond Hill's Heritage. A Guide for Teachers.* 1979.

Mitchell, John. *The Settlement of York County.* York County: The Municipal Corporation of the County of York, 1950.

National Archives of Canada, Historical Resources Branch, Economic and Transportation Unit, State, Military and Transportation Records Government Archives Division. *Record Group 3, Records of the Post Office, Series D.3., Divisional Inspectors' Reports.*

"Proposed New Bond Lake Sub-division Has Interesting Historical Background." *Aurora Banner,* June 21, 1956.

"Quetton St. George." *Aurora Banner,* May 6, 1938.

Richardson, Marjorie E. "A 'Quick' History of Whitchurch Township," 1975.

Roberts, Helen. "Rural Schools of Whitchurch." Whitchurch-Stouffville Museum, 1985–1992.

Scadding, Henry. *Toronto of Old: Collections and Recollections.* Toronto: Adam, Stevenson & Co, 1873.

Aurora

Johnston, James, M.A., Ph.D. *Aurora, Its Early Beginnings.* Aurora: Aurora Centennial Committee, 1963; 2nd edition, Aurora: Aurora & District Historical Society, 1972.

A Place in Time: Aurora's First Century of Settlement. Aurora: Aurora Heritage Committee, 1985.

A Summary of the Historical Development of York Region. The Regional Municipality of York, Regional Official Plan, Technical Appendix 1, June 1974.

Newmarket

Byers, Mary, Jan Kennedy, Margaret McBurney, and the Junior League of Toronto. *Rural Roots.* Toronto: University of Toronto Press, 1976.

Carter, Terry. *The Market Square Plaques.* Newmarket: Newmarket Historical Society, 1992.

de Zwaan, George. "Elite and Society: Newmarket, Ontario 1857–1880." M.A. Thesis, Queen's University, Kingston, 1980.

Roberts, Helen. "Rural Schools of Whitchurch." Whitchurch-Stouffville Museum, 1985–1992.

Smith, W. Randy. "The Early Development of Three Upper Canadian Towns: Barrie, Holland Landing and Newmarket." Discussion Paper No. 16, Department of Geography, York University, 1977.

Trewhella, Ethel Wilson. *History of the Town of Newmarket.* N.p., n.d.

White Rose

Aurora Banner, May 9, 1873

Aurora Banner, April 2, 1956

Gormley Women's Institute. Deed: S. Siddons to Trustees of S. S. # 6.

———. "Tweedsmuir History Book." N.d.

History of Toronto and County of York, Ontario. Vol. II. Toronto: C. Blackett Robinson, 1885.

Illustrated Historical Atlas of the County of York. Selected and reprinted from original 1878 edition. Toronto: Peter Martin Associates Ltd., 1969.

National Archives of Canada, Historical Resources Branch, Economic and Transportation Unit, State, Military and Transportation Records Government Archives Division. *Record Group 3, Records of the Post Office, Series D.3., Divisional Inspectors' Reports.*

Richardson, Marjorie E. "A History of Petchville." Ca. 1988.

Tremaine, George R. *Tremaine's Map of the County of York Canada West.* Toronto: George C. Tremaine, 1860.

Vandorf Women's Institute. "Tweedsmuir History Book." N.d.

Petchville

Aurora Banner. May 31, 1872.

Aurora Banner. July 18, 1973.

Aurora Banner. May 9, 1890.

Aurora Banner. June 27, 1890.

Aurora Banner. July 25, 1890.

Byers, Mary, Jan Kennedy, Margaret McBurney, and the Junior League of Toronto. *Rural Roots.* Toronto: University of Toronto Press, 1976.

Illustrated Historical Atlas of the County of York. Selected and reprinted from original 1878 edition. Toronto: Peter Martin Associates Ltd., 1969.

Richardson, Marjorie E. "A History of Petchville." N.d.

Stuart, Jacqueline. "Brief: House at the South-East Corner of Wellington and Leslie Streets Aurora–Lot 20 Concession Three, East of Yonge St." Aurora and District Historical Museum, rev. February 1991.

Tremaine, George R. *Tremaine's Map of the County of York Canada West.* Toronto: George C. Tremaine, 1860.

Bogarttown

Bogarttown Women's Institute. "Tweedsmuir History Book." N.d.

"The Founding of Bogart Town." *Newmarket Era*, 1938.

Richardson, Marjorie E. "Research Item 2." January 14, 1971.

———. "Whitchurch Township—County—York." N.d.

Roberts, Helen. "Rural Schools of Whitchurch." Whitchurch-Stouffville Museum, 1985–1992.

Starr, Elmer. "History of the Hamlet of Bogarttown." 1948.

Starr, Leonora. "Lot 30, Concession 2, William and Frances Walker." N.d.

Tremaine, George R. *Tremaine's Map of the County of York Canada West*. Toronto: George C. Tremaine, 1860.

Gormley

Byers, Mary, Jan Kennedy, Jan, Margaret McBurney, and the Junior League of Toronto. *Rural Roots*. Toronto: University of Toronto Press, 1976.

Champion, Isabel, ed. *Markham 1793–1900*. Markham: Markham Historical Society, 1979.

Champion, Mary B., ed. *Markham Remembered*. Markham: Markham Historical Society, 1988.

Cober, Pastor James, Mary Cober, Rev. Henry Heise, and Bruce Vander Bent. *100 Years at Heise Hill Church, Centennial History, 1877–1977*. The Centennial Committee, 1977.

Gormley Women's Institute. "Tweedsmuir History Book." N.d.

Moorby, Mrs. Mossie. Newmarket, Ontario. Interview.

National Archives of Canada, Historical Resources Branch, Economic and Transportation Unit, State, Military and Transportation Records Government Archives Division. *Record Group 3, Records of the Post Office, Series D.3., Divisional Inspectors' Reports*.

Preston Lake

Carter, Floreen Ellen. *Place Names of Ontario*. London, Ontario: Phelps Publishing Company, 1984.

Hennessey, Lorne. Vandorf, Ontario. Interview. December 1985.

Illustrated Historical Atlas of the County of York. Selected and reprinted from original 1878 edition. Toronto: Peter Martin Associates Ltd., 1969.

Ontario Ministry of Consumer and Commercial Relations, Land Registry Office, Newmarket. Abstracts for: Lot 11, Concession 4, Lot 12, Concession 4.

Preston, Rick. Preston Lake, Ontario. Interview. March 1993.

Richardson, Marjorie E. "Century Farms of Whitchurch-Stouffville." April 1967.

———. Vandorf, Ontario. Interview. December 1985.

Whitchurch Township Map, Original Land Grant Holders, 1805–1857.

Pleasantville

Bogarttown Women's Institute. "Tweedsmuir History Book." N.d.

Historical Sketch of Whitchurch-Stouffville. Centennial Celebration of Municipal Government 1850–1950. Township of Whitchurch, 1950.

National Archives of Canada, Historical Resources Branch, Economic and Transportation Unit, State, Military and Transportation Records Government Archives Division. *Record Group 3, Records of the Post Office, Series D.3., Divisional Inspectors' Reports*.

"Our Hamlets Then and Now." *Stouffville Sun*, January 8, 1986, 12.

Tremaine, George R. *Tremaine's Map of the County of York Canada West*. Toronto: George C. Tremaine, 1860.

Bethesda

Atkinson, Clarence, Selina Atkinson, Len Brillinger, and Clifford Burkholder. "Bethesda United Church Centennial Anniversary September 25th to October 2nd 1955." 1955.

Bethesda Women's Institute. "Tweedsmuir History Book." N.d.

Bruce, A.D. *History of the Bethesda and Stouffville Telephone Company*. *Stouffville Tribune*, 1958.

Clubine, Egerton. Kitchener, Ontario. Interview. April 1986.

"Our Hamlets Then and Now." *Stouffville Sun*, February 5, 1986, 15.

Town of Whitchurch-Stouffville, Ontario. Whitchurch-Stouffville Museum. Selina Atkinson Memoirs.

Pine Orchard and Cedar Valley

Census Records, 1851–81.

Illustrated Historical Atlas of the County of York. Selected and reprinted from original 1878 edition. Toronto: Peter Martin Associates Ltd., 1969.

Johnston, Beatrice. Interview.

Johnston, Helen. Interview.

Macklem, Nora. "Memoirs" (private collection). 1968.

"Our Hamlets Then and Now." *Stouffville Sun*, October 23, 1985, 16, and December 18, 1985, 10.

Pine Orchard Women's Institute. "Tweedsmuir History Book." N.d.

Stephens, Alma. Interview.

Tremaine, George R. *Tremaine's Map of the County of York Canada West*. Toronto: George C. Tremaine, 1860.

Lemonville

Cook, Earl. Lemonville, Ontario. Interview. October 1991.

Kirby, Ken. Stouffville, Ontario. Interview. October 1991.

Pipher, Cliff. Stouffville, Ontario. Interview. 1930–1940.

Pipher, Mel. Stouffville, Ontario. Interview. 1950.

Pipher, Walter. Stouffville, Ontario. Interview. June 1988.

Shrubmount

Canada and its Provinces, Province of Ontario Pt. 1. Vol. 17. Shortt & Goughty, 1914.

"Our Hamlets Then and Now," *Stouffville Sun,* May 21, 1986, 14.

Reaman, George E. *Trail of the Black Walnut.* Toronto: McClelland & Stewart, 1957.

Rolling, Gladys. *East Gwillimbury in the Nineteenth Century.* Toronto: Ryerson Press, 1969.

Ringwood

Wideman, Enoch Martin, and Norman E. Wideman. "Wideman Family History in Canada and United States." 1955.

Yakely, Florence Brownsberger. "Ringwood." *Canadian-German Folklore. More Pioneer Hamlets of York.* Vol. 9. 1985.

Ballantrae

Byers, Mary, Jan Kennedy, Margaret McBurney, and the Junior League of Toronto. *Rural Roots.* Toronto: University of Toronto Press, 1976.

Census Records, 1851–81.

Cooper, Charles. *Narrow Gauge for Us, The Story of the Toronto and Nipissing Railway.* Erin, Ontario: The Boston Mills Press, n.d.

History of Toronto and County of York, Ontario. Vol II. Toronto: C. Blackett Robinson, 1885.

Illustrated Historical Atlas of the County of York. Selected and reprinted from original 1878 edition. Toronto: Peter Martin Associates Ltd., 1969.

McKinley, W. Ballantrae, Ontario. Interview.

"Our Hamlets Then and Now." *Stouffville Sun,* November 6, 1985, 32.

Vivian

Census Records, 1851–81.

Cooper, Charles. *Narrow Gauge for Us, The Story of the Toronto and Nipissing Railway.* Erin, Ontario: The Boston Mills Press, n.d.

Illustrated Historical Atlas of the County of York. Selected and reprinted from original 1878 edition. Toronto: Peter Martin Associates Ltd., 1969.

"Our Hamlets Then and Now," *Stouffville Sun,* February 12, 1986, 13.

Mitchell, John. *The Settlement of York County.* York County: The Municipal Corporation of the County of York, 1950.

Reaman, George E. *Trail of the Black Walnut.* Toronto: McClelland & Stewart, 1957.

Hartman

Canada and Its Provinces, Province of Ontario Pt. 1. Vol. 17. Shortt & Goughty, 1914.

Census Records, 1851–81.

de Zwaan, George. "Elite and Society, Newmarket 1857–1880." Thesis, Queen's University, Kingston, Ontario, 1980.

History of Toronto and County of York. Vol. II. Toronto: C. Blackett Robinson, 1885.

Illustrated Historical Atlas of the County of York. Selected and reprinted from original 1878 edition. Toronto: Peter Martin Associates Ltd., 1969.

Martin, John. *The Settlement of York County.* York County: The Municipal Corporation of the County of York, 1950.

Oldham, Mrs. J. Interview.

"Our Hamlets Then and Now." *Stouffville Sun,* May 21, 1986, 14.

Rolling, Gladys. *East Gwillimbury in the Nineteenth Century.* Toronto: Ryerson Press, 1969.

Stouffville

Hoover, Edna. Stouffville, Ontario. Interview. November 1991.

Hoover, Eva. Stouffville, Ontario. Interview. May 1980.

Mertens, Margery. "Memoirs." 1927.

Stouffer, David. "Memoirs." 1927.

Stouffville Women's Institute. "Tweedsmuir History Book." N.d.

van Smerison, Henry. Diary (private collection). 1850–60.

Bloomington

"Brief Church Items." *Christian Guardian,* 1882, 13.

Burnett, Vera, and Gertrude Otto. "Bloomington History." 1963.

Carter, Floreen Ellen. *Place Names of Ontario.* London, Ontario: Phelps Publishing Company, 1984.

Census Records, 1861 and 1871.

Clubine, Egerton. Kitchener, Ontario. Interview. April 1986.

Harding, Meeda. Stouffville, Ontario. Interview. November, 1988.

Illustrated Historical Atlas of the County of York. Selected and reprinted from original 1878 edition. Toronto: Peter Martin Associates Ltd., 1969.

Lemon, Eugene. Bloomington, Ontario. Interview. November 1985.

National Archives of Canada, Historical Resources Branch, Economic and Transportation Unit, State, Military and Transportation Records Government Archives Division. *Record Group 3, Records of the Post Office, Series D.3., Divisional Inspectors' Reports.*

Ontario Ministry of Consumer and Commercial Relations, Land Registry Office, Newmarket. Abstracts for: Lot 9, Concession 8, Lot 10, Concession 8, Lot 10, Concession 9 west.

Richardson, Marjorie E. "Century Farms of Whitchurch-Stouffville." April 1967.

Whitchurch Township Map of Original Land Grant Holders 1802–57.

Musselman's Lake
Barkey, Jean. Stouffville, Ontario. Interview. January 1986.

Carter, Floreen Ellen. *Place Names of Ontario.* London, Ontario: Phelps Publishing Company, 1984.

Census Records, 1861 and 1871.

Christian Church Cemetery (Churchill). Toronto: Ontario Genealogical Society, Toronto Branch, 1990.

Coultice, Jim. Musselman's Lake. Interview. January 1986.

Davies, Audrey and Vern. Musselman's Lake. Interview, September 1990.

Davies, George. Musselman's Lake. Interview. January 1986.

Illustrated Historical Atlas of the County of York. Selected and reprinted from original 1878 edition. Toronto: Peter Martin Associates Ltd., 1969.

Jenkins, Gwen. Untitled Pamphlet of Lake History. 1974.

Lamb, Marjorie, and Barry Pearson. *The Boyd Gang.* Toronto: Peter Martin Associates, 1976.

National Archives of Canada, Historical Resources Branch, Economic and Transportation Unit, State, Military and Transportation Records Government Archives Division. *Record Group 3, Records of the Post Office, Series D.3., Divisional Inspectors' Reports.*

Ontario Ministry of Consumer and Commercial Relations, Land Registry Office, Newmarket. Abstracts for: Lot 16, Concession 8, Lot 17, Concession 8, Lot 18, Concession 8, Lot 19, Concession 8.

Reaman, G. Elmore. *A History of Vaughan Township.* Toronto: University of Toronto Press, 1971.

Whitchurch Township Map of Original Land Grants 1802–57.

Churchill
"Brief Church Items." *Christian Guardian,* January 11, 1882, 13.

Carter, Floreen Ellen. *Place Names of Ontario.* London, Ontario: Phelps Publishing Company, 1984.

Census Records, 1861 and 1871.

Christian Church Cemetery (Churchill). Toronto: Ontario Genealogical Society, Toronto Branch, 1990.

"Churchill Church." No author, n.p., n.d.

Degeer, Osborne. Ballantrae, Ontario. Interview. November 1991.

Harding, Meeda. Stouffville, Ontario. Interview. November 1991.

Illustrated Historical Atlas of the County of York. Selected and reprinted from original 1878 edition. Toronto: Peter Martin Associates Ltd., 1969.

McGillivray, Allan. Zephyr, Ontario. Interview. March 1986.

McLaughlin, Carrie. Churchill, Ontario. Interview. March 1986.

Ontario Ministry of Consumer and Commercial Relations, Land Registry Office, Newmarket. Abstracts for: Lot 20, Concession 8, Lot 21, Concession 8, Lot 20, Concession 9, Lot 21, Concession 9.

Paisley, Eugene. Stouffville, Ontario. Interview. March 1986.

Pegg, Milton Newton. "Genealogy of the Hill Family That Came From County Tyrone, Ireland, and Settled in Whitchurch Township, York County, Ontario, in 1812." June 2, 1969.

Whitchurch Township Map of Original Land Grants 1802–57.

Lincolnville
Cook, Blanche. Lemonville, Ontario. Interview. November 1991.

Thomas, Mel. Stouffville, Ontario. Interview. October 1991.

Thomas, Muriel. Stouffville, Ontario. Interview. October 1991.

Island Lake
Broad, Bill. Island Lake, Ontario. Interview. March 1986.

Census Records, 1861 and 1871.

Illustrated Historical Atlas of the County of York. Selected and reprinted from original 1878 edition. Toronto: Peter Martin Associates Ltd., 1969.

McGillivray, Allan. Zephyr, Ontario. Interview. March 1986.

Ontario Ministry of Consumer and Commercial Relations, Land Registry Office, Newmarket. Abstracts for: Lot 20, Concession 8, Lot 21, Concession 8, Lot 19, Concession 8.

Paisley, Eugene. Stouffville, Ontario. Interview. March 1986.

Whitchurch Township Map of Original Land Grants 1802–57.

CHAPTER 5: Physical Geography
Dreimanis, Aleksis. "Late Wisconsin Glacial Retreat in the Great Lakes Region, North America." Edited by Walter S. Newman and Bert Salwin. Annals of the New York Academy of Sciences, Vol. 288.

Hewitt, D.F. *Industrial Minerals of the Markham-Newmarket Area.* Industrial Mineral Report 24. Toronto: Ontario Department of Mines, 1969.

Hoffman, D.W., and N.R. Richards. *Soil Survey of York County.* Canada Department of Agriculture and Ontario Agricultural College, Report No: 19 of the Ontario Soil Survey, 1954.

Karrow, P.F., and B.G. Warner. "The Geological and Biological Environment for Human Occupation in Southern Ontario." In Chris J. Ellis and Neal Ferris, ed. *The Archaeology of Southern*

Ontario to A.D. 1650. London, Ontario: Occasional Publication of the London Chapter, OAS Number 5,1990.

Liberty, Bruce. *Palaeozoic Geology of the Lake Simcoe Area, Ontario*. Geological Survey of Canada, Memoir 355. Department of Energy, Mines and Resources Canada, 1969.

McAndrews, J.H. "Fossil Pollen and Our Changing Landscape and Climate." *Rotunda*, Spring, 1970.

Webber, L.R. and D.W. Hoffman. *Origin, Classification and Use of Ontario Soils*. Guelph: Department of Soil Science, Ontario Agricultural College, University of Guelph, n.d.

CHAPTER 6: Archaeology

Adam, G.M. and C.P. Mulvany. *Toronto and the County of York, Ontario. Vol.* I. Toronto: C. Blackett Robinson, Publisher, 1885.

Annette, Sister M., CPS. *Salute to Canada*. Oak Ridges: Our Lady of Annunciation School, 1967.

Archaeological Services Inc. *First Annual Archaeological Report, Ontario (New Series) 1990*. Ontario Heritage Foundation, 1991.

Barkey, Jean, comp. *A Pictorial History of a Prosperous Ontario Community, Stouffville: 1877–1977*. Stouffville: The Bryant Press, 1977.

Bonnycastle, Sir Richard S. *The Canadas in 1841*. Vol. 2. S.R. Publishers Limited, Johnson Reprint Corporation, 1968.

Burgar, Robert W.C. *An Archaeological Master Plan for the Metropolitan Toronto and Region Conservation Authority*. Downsview: M.T.R.C.A., 1990.

Calef, George. *Caribou and the Barren-lands*. Scarborough: Firefly Books Limited, 1981.

Carter, Terry. Former editor of *Newmarket Era*. Personal Communication, 1978.

Chewett, William. (copy). Outline of Some Townships Between Lakes Ontario and Simcoe. Upper Canada. Office of the Surveyor General, ca. 1799. Archives of Ontario.

Chewett, W. to E.B. Littlehales. (Concerning a letter by W. Bond) In Cruikshank, E.A., ed. *The Correspondence of Lieut. Governor John Graves Simcoe*. Vol. 3. Toronto: Ontario Historical Society, 1925.

Deller, D. Brian. "The Paleo-Indian Occupations of Southwestern Ontario: Distribution, Technology and Social Organization." Ph.d. Dissertation, Department of Anthropology, McGill University, 1988.

Dibb, Gordon C. "An Archaeological Survey of the East Holland River and Its Environs." Report on File with the Ontario Ministry of Citizenship and Culture, Toronto, 1979.

———. "Boyd Conservation Area Survey and Upper Nursery Site Test Excavations: 1981." Report Prepared for the Metropolitan Toronto and Area Conservation Authority, Downsview, 1982.

———. "Late Palaeo-Indian Settlement Patterns Along the Margins of the Simcoe Lowlands in Southern Ontario." M.A. Thesis, Department of Anthropology, Trent University, Peterborough, 1985.

Eid, Leroy. "The Ojibwa-Iroquois War: The War the Five Nations Did Not Win." *Ethnohistory*, 26/4, 1979.

Ellis, Chris J., and D. Brian Deller. "Paleo-Indians." In Chris J. Ellis and Neal Ferris, ed. *The Archaeology of Southern Ontario to A.D. 1650*. Occasional Publication of the London Chapter, OAS. Number 5, 1990.

Ellis, Chris J., Ian T. Kenyon, and Michael Spence. "The Archaic." In Chris J. Ellis and Neal Ferris, ed. *The Archaeology of Southern Ontario to A.D. 1650*. Occasional Publication of the London Chapter, OAS. Number 5, 1990.

Gentilcore, L., and C.G. Head. *Ontario History in Maps*. Toronto: University of Toronto Press, 1984.

Heidenreich, Conrad. *Huronia: A History and Geography of the Huron Indians, 1600–1650*. Toronto: McClelland & Stewart, 1973.

Jamieson, S. Trent University. Personal communication, 1990.

Johnson, Leo A. *The History of the County of Ontario: 1615–1875*. Whitby: The Corporation of the County of Ontario, 1973.

Johnston, Richard B. "Archaeology of the Serpent Mounds Site." Royal Ontario Museum, Art and Archaeology Occasional Paper 10, 1968.

Kapches, Mima. "The Middleport Pattern in Ontario Iroquoian Prehistory." Ph.d. Dissertation, University of Toronto, 1981.

Kenyon, Walter. "The Miller Site." Royal Ontario Museum, Art and Archaeology, Occasional Paper 14, 1968.

Kidd, Kenneth. "Burial Site at Ringwood, Ontario." Report on File with the Department of New World Archaeology, Royal Ontario Museum, Toronto, 1954.

McAndrews, J.H., and L.J. Jackson. "Age and Environment of Late Pleistocene Mastodon and Mammoth in Southern Ontario." In R.S. Lamb, N. Miller and D. Steadman, ed. *Late Pleistocene and Early Holocene Paleoecology of the Eastern Great Lakes Region*. Bulletin of the Buffalo Society of Natural Sciences, Vol. 33, 1988.

McGreevy, Thomas. "Faunal Analysis of the Ratcliffe Site (AlGt-157)." Anthropology Term Paper on File with the Department of Anthropology, University of Toronto, 1981.

McIlwraith, Thomas F. "The Adequacy of Rural Roads in the Era Before Railways: An Illustration from Upper Canada." In Graeme Wynn, ed. *People Places Patterns Processes: Geographical Perspectives on the Canadian Past*. Toronto: Copp Clark Pitman Ltd., 1990.

McNeish, R.S. *Iroquois Pottery Types*. National Museum of Canada, Bulletin 124.

Noble, W.C. "The Sopher Celt: An Indicatory of Early Protohistoric Trade in Huronia." *Ontario Archaeology*, Vol. 16, 42–47.

Patterson, George C. "Land Settlement in Upper Canada, 1783–1840." *Sixteenth Report of the Department of Archives for the Province of Ontario*. 1921.

Ramsden, Peter. "A Refinement of Some Aspects of Huron Ceramic Analysis." National Museum of Man, Archaeological Survey of Canada Paper No. 63, 1977.

———. "Rich Man, Poor Man, Dead Man, Thief: The Dispersal of Wealth in 17th Century Huronia." *Ontario Archaeology*, Vol. 35, 35–40.

Ritchie, William. *A Typology and Nomenclature for New York Projectile Points*. Personal Edition. New York Museum of Science Services, Bulletin 384, 1971.

Smith, Donald B. "The Dispossession of the Mississauga Indians: A Missing Chapter in the Early History of Upper Canada." *Ontario History*, June 1981, 76.

Spence, Michael, Robert H. Phil, and Carl R. Murphy. "Cultural Complexes of the Early and Middle Woodland Periods." In Chris J. Ellis and Neal Ferris, ed. *The Archaeology of Southern Ontario to A.D. 1650*. Occasional Publications of the London Chapter, OAS. Number 5, 1990.

Storck, Peter L. "Recent Excavations at the Udora Site: A Gainey/Clovis Occupation Site in Southern Ontario." *Current Research in the Pleistocene*. Vol. 5, 1988.

———. "Research into the Paleo-Indian Occupations of Ontario: A Review." *Ontario Archaeology*, Vol. 41, 1984, 3–28.

Trewhella, Ethel Wilson. *History of the Town of Newmarket*. N.p., n.d.

van Nostrand, Dr. F.H. "Vandorf: Prehistoric and Early Historic Times–Land, Water, Trees and People." Possession of van Nostrand Family, Vandorf. N.d.

Williams, Pat. "Faunal Analysis of the Ratcliffe Site." Term Paper on File with the Department of Anthropology, University of Toronto, 1983.

Wright, J.V. *The Ontario Iroquois Tradition*. National Museum of Canada Bulletin 210, 1973.

———. *The Shield Archaic*. National Museums of Canada, Publications in Archaeology Number 3, 1972.

Appendix A: Churches

Atkinson, Clarence, Selina Atkinson, Len Brillinger, and Clifford Burkholder. "Bethesda United Church Centennial Anniversary September 25 to October 2nd." 1955.

Aurora United Church 150th Anniversary Committee. *150th Anniversary of the Founding and Dedication of Aurora United Church 1818–1968*.

Barkey, Jean. *A Pictorial History of a Prosperous Ontario Community, Stouffville: 1877–1977*. Stouffville: The Bryant Press, 1977.

Centennial Committee of Christ Church. *Christ Church Stouffville. The First Century 1879–1979*.

Christian Church Cemetery (Churchill). Toronto: Ontario Genealogical Society, Toronto Branch, 1990.

"Churchill Church." No author, n.p., n.d.

"Churchill Church Centennial." 1872–1972. No author, n.p., n.d.

Cober, Pastor James, Mary Cober, Rev. Henry Heise, and Bruce Vander Bent. *100 Years at Heise Hill Church, Centennial History 1877–1977*. The Centennial Committee, 1977.

Gormley Women's Institute. "Tweedsmuir History Book." N.d.

"History of the Churches of Stouffville." November 1943. No author.

Johnston, James. *Aurora Its Early Beginnings*. Aurora: Aurora Centennial Committee, 1963; 2nd Edition Aurora: Aurora and District Historical Society, 1972.

Otto, Gertrude, and Vera Burnett. "Bloomington Churches." N.d.

Richardson, Marjorie E. "Lemonville in the 1800s." N.d.

"Ringwood Congregational Christian Church 1824–1974." No author, n.d.

Rush, Margaret E., and Marjorie Richardson. "Baker Hill Baptist Church and Cemetery." *Canadian Genealogist*, Vol. 1, No. 1, 1979.

Somerville, Patricia, and Catherine MacFarlane. *A History of Vaughan Township Churches*. Vaughan Township Historical Society, 1984.

"Stouffville Missionary Church." Service of Dedication, May 31, 1987. No author.

Trewhella, Ethel Wilson. *History of the Town of Newmarket*, n.p., n.d.

United Church Archives, Victoria University Archives, Victoria University. In the University of Toronto, Toronto, Ontario.

Wood, Udelle V., comp. "Memorial Christian Church 150th Anniversary Stouffville, Ontario 1842–1992."

———. "Our Christian Heritage." 1991.

Appendix B: Schools

Roberts, Helen. "Rural Schools of Whitchurch." Whitchurch-Stouffville Museum, 1985–1992.

Appendix C: Municipal Government

Department of Municipal Affairs. AO RG19. *Minutes and By-laws, County of York 1877–1961*. Archives of Ontario.

———. AO RG21. *Minutes and By-laws, Village of Stouffville 1877–1970*. Archives of Ontario.

———. *Municipal Financial Returns 1879–1945*. (Box 705) Archives of Ontario.

Illustrated Historical Atlas of the County of York. Selected and reprinted from original 1878 edition. Toronto: Peter Martin Associates Ltd., 1969.

Newmarket Era. 1852–1971.
Stouffville Tribune. 1888–1993.

Appendix D: Post Offices
National Archives of Canada, Historical Resources Branch, Economic and Transportation Unit, State, Military and Transportation Records Government Archives Division. *Record Group 3, Records of the Post Office, Series D. 3., Divisional Inspectors' Reports.*

Appendix E: Summary of Forest Products—1861 Census
The Ontario Census for Whitchurch Township, 1871.

Appendix F: Summary of Sawmill Statistics—1861 Census
The Canada West Census for Whitchurch Township, 1861.

SOURCES

The following is a list of sources employed in both primary and secondary research.

Libraries and Archives
Aurora Public Library
Bell Canada
Bloomington Cemetery
CN Archives
Canada Post
Census Records (Whitchurch) 1851–1891
Lake Simcoe Region Conservation Authority
Metropolitan Toronto and Region Conservation Authority
Metropolitan Toronto Reference Library
National Archives of Canada
Newmarket Historical Society Archives
Ontario Hydro
Ontario Ministry of Consumer and Commercial Relations, Land Registry Office, Newmarket
Ontario Ministry of Natural Resources
Pickering College Library/Archives
Provincial Archives of Ontario
Synopsis of Public Schools Inspectors' Reports for the Northern Division of York 1851, 1868, 1870 (Provincial Archives of Ontario)
Toronto City Archives
United Church of Canada Archives
Whitchurch-Stouffville Museum Archives
Whitchurch-Stouffville Public Library
York Region Board of Education Archives

Newspapers
Aurora Banner, April 12, 1872–December 7, 1877
Free Press Weekly, January 1889–December 1889
Newmarket Era, 1852–1900
Pilot Paper, January 1889–December 1889
Stouffville Tribune, 1888–1939

MAPS LEGEND

———————		Lot Line
══════════		Roads and highways
–·–·–·–		Railroad
⊠	PO	Post Office
⦂⦂⦂⦂		Orchards
⊕	SM	Sawmill
	GM	Grist Mill
		Mill
⊡		School
		Brickyard

☆ Carriage Factory
Cheese Factory
Foundry
Hat Factory
Implement Factory
Potash Works
Shingle Factory
Stove Factory
Tannery
Woollen factory
† Cemetery
□ House
▢ Hotel
▲ Tavern

★ Churches:

Bap	Baptist
C	Congregational
CC	Christian Conference Baptist
CE	Church of England
E	Episcopal
M	Methodist
PM	Primitive Methodist
WM	Wesleyan Methodist
Pres	Presbyterian
RC	Roman Catholic

INDEX